SPORTS CAR
AND
COMPETITION DRIVING

Sports Car
and
Competition Driving

◆

Paul Frère

◆

1963
ROBERT BENTLEY, Inc
993 Massachusetts Avenue
Cambridge 38, Massachusetts

First published 1963

© *Paul Frère 1963*

PRINTED AND BOUND IN GREAT BRITAIN BY JARROLD AND SONS LTD
LONDON AND NORWICH

PREFACE

I DO not believe that any book, or any amount of training of the kind given in competition driving courses, will make a good driver of anyone who does not possess a fundamental, inborn aptitude. Above a certain level, driving becomes a sport, demanding of its adepts instant and accurate reflexes combined with perfect judgement. In this sphere, only those who enjoy an outstanding natural gift, and who take a profound interest in the subject, will ever reach the top.

For this reason, I had some hesitation before writing this book—I thought, for instance, of Stirling Moss, Mike Hawthorn, Tony Brooks or Jim Clark, who all started winning races in their very first season of serious racing, at an age when they could have had comparatively little driving experience at all. But surely, they are exceptions, and between the two extremes of the born champion and the hopeless incompetent, there must be hundreds of good drivers who, even if they cannot hope to emulate potential world champions, might gain immense satisfaction from taking part in all sorts of motoring events.

These are the non-professionals who, as a rule, cannot devote much time to their motoring activities and who will surely greatly benefit from all the experience that can be passed on to them, thereby reducing the time necessary for satisfying results to be achieved, in whatever sort of competition they intend to enter. If they have analytical minds, they will probably also like to have a better knowledge of the basic physics governing the behaviour and the attitude of their car on the road, which, in turn, will help them drive it to better purpose.

The greater part of this book deals with racing, rather than rallying or any other sort of competition in which a time element is involved. This is not only because I consider circuit racing to be motor sport in its purest form (where few factors other than achieving the highest possible speed over a given distance are involved) but also because all the general rules of racing apply, basically, to any other sort of driving—after incidentals such as lack of previous knowledge of the road and the presence on it of other traffic and so on, have been taken into account.

I therefore think that a better knowledge and understanding of the factors involved in competition driving should be of benefit to *any* driver, even if he does not take part in any sort of competition, and thereby contributes to greater safety on the road.

P. F.

Brussels,
January 1963

CONTENTS

ACKNOWLEDGMENT

THE Author and the Publishers are indebted to the following for supplying the illustrations in this book:

Aston Martin Lagonda Ltd., for fig. 50; André Van Bever, Brussels, for figs. 1–9, 11–14, 19–21, 39–42, 47, 48, 51–5, 57 and 58; Geoffrey Goddard, for fig. 56; Halda Ltd., for fig. 46; Ed. Heuer and Co. S.A., Bienne, for fig. 44; Louis Klemantaski, for fig. 10; Les Leston Ltd., for figs. 45 and 49; Max Pichler, Zurich, for fig. 22.

The remainder of the illustrations were specially prepared for the book by P. Weller.

LIST OF ILLUSTRATIONS

The numerals in parentheses in the text refer to the *figure numbers*
of illustrations

9

CHAPTER I

CONTROLS

LEARN to be a good driver first!

Who is a good driver and who is not is a matter for discussion. Obviously, your family would not like you to drive them to the holiday resort of their choice in the same way you would drive in a big rally or in a race. One day, while I was away racing somewhere in Europe, my wife and my children were driven home from friends living out in the provinces by a quiet gentleman using a big American car. Arriving home, the children said to their mother, 'How nice it is to be driven in such a smooth and quiet way; what a pity father doesn't drive as well as this gentleman!' But even if the sort of driving that is best suited to a Sunday outing is not exactly what is required of a racing driver, there are general rules that must be applied by both types—the observance of which, distinguish the better from the not-so-good driver.

Driving Position

One of the basic requirements of good driving is a comfortable and purposeful driving position. Not many drivers are fully aware of its extreme importance, for it not only makes long journeys more comfortable but also improves the precision and the rapidity of their control of the car.

The body must be well supported, yet at the same time the position must afford complete freedom to perform those movements which are normally required in driving. The driver must be able to push all the pedals down firmly, without moving the body, and his right foot must be able to move quickly from the accelerator pedal to the brake pedal without the steering wheel fouling his knees. Ideally it should be possible for this movement to be carried out without moving the leg at all. The arms must be perfectly free to allow for movements of large amplitude.

In my opinion, the most important point about the driving

position is that the distance between the driver and the steering wheel should be adequate. Most drivers sit too near the wheel because, when they were novices, they thought that by sitting near to the windscreen, they could better judge the width of their car and see the road better, and they have never thought of changing this position since. In actual fact, it does not matter a bit if you can see the road a few inches nearer the car or not, and very soon a driver learns to know where the nearside of his car is without actually seeing it. The latter point, moreover, does not apply to most modern cars where the nearside is plainly visible however far back the driver sits.

If you make a driver sit farther back, he will most probably protest that he does not feel as safe as he did before. But that feeling will soon disappear and he will quickly become a better driver just because he is sitting in a better position. One of the reasons for this is that by sitting farther back he will not be able to brace himself by the steering wheel on corners. This will improve the precision of his control and will give him a finer feel of the road.

However, the main reason why a driver should sit well away from the wheel is that this position gives him a much better freedom of movement. From the normal position where his hands are poised at about 'a quarter to three' on the steering wheel, he can turn it for roughly half a turn either way without the lower hand or arm fouling either the back of the seat or his body, and still keep complete control over the steering. For better sensitivity and precision, the hands should be lightly poised on the wheel, perhaps with one thumb holding a spoke for a safer grip, but never should the wheel be gripped tightly.

There is a strong tendency among drivers to use the steering wheel as a brace against the centrifugal force on bends and corners—a habit which prohibits any sensitivity of feeling for the steering. Instead, the driver should sit well back, and if necessary actually dig himself into the seat-back by pushing his body into it with his left foot, so as to get firm lateral support without the aid of the wheel.

A light grip on the wheel is so important that the late Mike Hawthorn always insisted on having a four-spoke steering wheel so that he could keep his hands in the proper position just by hooking his thumbs around the horizontal spokes. In a racing car, of course, the driver always gets much better lateral support than in a normal touring car anyway, because racing cars always have

1 Correct position at the wheel—the arms are well extended, the hands poised on the rim. A slight hold of the thumbs on the spokes may help towards gripping the wheel lightly. The seat back is inclined well rearward, giving good support

2 Incorrect position at the wheel—the driver is sitting too near the wheel, restricting the arms' freedom of movement. The hands are gripping the wheel too tightly and must be held too high in order to enable them to move the wheel at all before the elbows make contact with the seat back. The squab is too upright, giving the body little support. The knees make too sharp an angle, so that the thighs lack support and the knees interfere with the wheel

3 *The distance between the seat and the wheel must be governed by the fact that, when the hand reaches the top of the wheel, the arm should be fully extended, but without it being necessary for the body to lean forward. Note that the lower hand easily clears the body*

4 *When the driver sits too close to the wheel, the lower hand interferes with the body and the elbow is pushed into the squab*

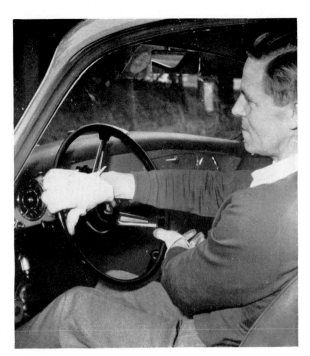

5, 6 From a correct position, the wheel can easily be moved over a full half-turn without the hands having to be shifted from their initial position . . .

. . . but if a sharp turn is expected, the hands should be moved on the rim beforehand, so that the wheel can be turned over a larger arc than from their initial, normal position. Better control over the car is afforded if, when the car is held in a corner, the hands and arms are in a near-normal position, than when they are crossed. If a very sharp turn makes it necessary to move the hands on the wheel during the turn, always turn the wheel over the largest possible arc in one single stroke

7 *From theory to practice: the author, driving a Formula II Cooper-Climax, sits well back, but has his left arm fully extended as he rounds a sharp corner*

8 *A perfect driving position illustrated by Olivier Gendebien on his way to his first Le Mans victory, in a Ferrari, in 1958*

properly designed bucket seats which are unsuitable for normal touring cars as they would make getting in and out too difficult.

Sitting back from the wheel can also be overdone. Never should the seat be moved so far back that the driver must actually lean forward in order to reach the top of the wheel, as this would reduce the lateral grip provided by the seat-back. The position I personally prefer is the one in which, without leaning forward at all, I can just reach the top of the steering wheel with my arms fully extended. The driving position should never be dictated by the distance away from the pedals. With the seat properly adjusted in relation to the steering wheel, there is very little chance that they will be too close. If they are too far away, they can be adjusted in some cars. If not, it is usually very easy to modify them, if only by screwing blocks of wood on to the pedal pads.

Once the fore-and-aft position of the seat is properly adjusted, attention should be paid to its height. This should be chosen so as to give maximum visibility without raising the seat to such an extent that the steering wheel interferes with the movements of the legs, or the thighs with the movements of the hands. In some cars the seats can be adjusted for height, in others a properly designed cushion may solve the problem. If the seat is to be permanently raised, however, it is better to modify its mountings than to use a cushion which was not originally designed for the seat and which will probably make it less comfortable on long runs.

Changing Gear

Changing gear used to be the greatest headache of novice drivers. Modern synchromesh gearboxes, however, have simplified the driver's task to such an extent that anyone is now able to change gear, at least without making horrible noises. Nevertheless, the way in which a gear change is executed, easily sorts out the good driver from the indifferent one. The difference lies much more in the way the clutch and accelerator pedals are used than in the way the gearbox itself is handled. It is well known that for a given road speed the engine runs at different speeds according to which gear is in use. Consequently, if a jerk is to be avoided when the driver lets the clutch in, after he has selected a new gear, the engine speed must be adjusted accordingly, before the clutch is re-engaged. This is very easy when selecting a higher gear, for instance changing from third to fourth, as in this case the time

17

necessary to move the lever from one position to the other usually just gives the engine a chance to slow down sufficiently for the drive to be taken up smoothly.

When a downward change is to be made, however, the engine must be accelerated while the change is being performed. Here, quite accurate judgement is necessary, as the engine must be accelerated by exactly the right amount if a jerk is to be avoided when the clutch is re-engaged. Moreover, if the down change is being performed in order to increase acceleration, or for climbing a hill, a smooth take-up can only be achieved if the engine is accelerated again while the drive is being taken up.

For this reason, in spite of modern synchronising devices, most good drivers continue to double de-clutch. This means that, when the gear lever has been moved into neutral, the clutch pedal is released for a brief moment while the engine is being accelerated before the clutch pedal is pushed in again and the next lower gear selected. This usually speeds up the engine by just the right amount for the drive to be taken up smoothly, besides nursing the synchromesh cones. In a racing car, double de-clutching is usually still a 'must', as very few of them use a synchromesh gearbox.

When to Change Gear

When to change gear depends very much on the objective. It may be maximum performance; it may be minimum consumption; it may also be minimum wear-and-tear on the car. These various aims call for differing techniques.

If minimum consumption is to be achieved you must remember that, in a petrol engine, the specific consumption decreases as the load on the engine is increased. This means that under given conditions and for a given speed of the car, the engine uses less petrol when it runs comparatively slowly—say in top gear—with a wide throttle opening than when it runs at a smaller throttle opening and at higher revolutions in a lower gear. It follows that to achieve the minimum fuel consumption, the engine must always be kept at the lowest possible revolution rate without, however, letting it drop into a range where efficiency is impaired. In this connection, it must be remembered that an engine's most efficient range of operation is the one over which it produces its maximum torque. Below this range the efficiency falls off again and the specific consumption rises, because the valve timing is not adapted to such low revolutions and losses occur due to scavenging of unburnt mixture and inadequate filling of the cylinders.

So, if maximum economy is the aim, gear changes must be performed in such a way that the engine is kept in the range where it produces its maximum torque provided this does not result in too high a maximum speed, when the increase in drag would offset the engine's low specific consumption.

For minimum wear-and-tear the engine should also be kept in the middle revolution ranges, but not be given full throttle unless it is running at least at half its maximum rotational speed. At fairly high revolutions, the inertia forces partly offset the high gas pressure resulting from full-throttle operation and transmitted to the bearings by the pistons and connecting rods. Very high rotational speeds, however, will result in very high inertia forces (which increase by the square of the rotational speed) with consequent high stresses on all moving parts. Slogging, or hard pulling, at low revolutions, will produce very high gas pressures and may also result in burnt valves while gas at high temperatures is laminated through them as they open and close comparatively slowly.

The main interest of the competition driver, however, lies in obtaining maximum performance. It is obvious that the higher the push the vehicle gets from its driving wheels, the faster will be its acceleration. The radius of the wheels being constant, the push will be proportional to the torque applied to the drive shafts. Neglecting the mechanical losses, this in turn will be equal to the torque produced by the engine multiplied by the gearbox ratio and multiplied again by the rear axle ratio (or front axle ratio if the car has front wheel drive). Thus, if the engine produces a torque of 100 lbs/ft which is put through a gearbox with a top gear ratio of 1:1 and through a rear axle with a ratio of 4:1, the torque on the wheel drive shafts will be 400 lbs/ft, and if the wheels have a radius of 1 foot the resulting push will be of 400 lbs. In fact, due to mechanical losses, this will be about 10% lower, that is about 360 lbs. In the following discussions, however, for simplicity's sake, we will disregard the mechanical losses, which increase slightly with the increase of the transmission ratio.

It is often said and written that, when trying to obtain maximum acceleration, there is no point in pushing the engine above its maximum torque range in the intermediate gears. This is entirely wrong, as it is easy to demonstrate.

Let us take the example of an engine that produces a fairly

constant maximum torque of 100 lbs/ft between 3,500 and 4,000 r.p.m. The torque then falls off to 85 lbs/ft at 5,000 r.p.m. and 72 lbs/ft at 5,500 r.p.m. which is the maximum speed at which the engine is allowed to run. Let us also suppose that the rear axle ratio is 4 : 1, that top gear is direct, giving a ratio of 1 : 1, and third gear has a ratio of 1·35 : 1, which results in an overall transmission ratio of 5·4 : 1. On this ratio, the maximum push that can be exerted by the driving wheels is

$$\frac{\text{torque} \times \text{overall gearing}}{\text{radius of the driving wheels}} = \frac{100 \times 5\cdot4}{1} = 540 \text{ lbs}$$

which is obtained between 3,500 and 4,000 r.p.m.

Having decided not to push the engine above the speed corresponding to the maximum torque output, we now change up into top gear, when the revolutions will drop to about 3,000 r.p.m. where a torque of only 96 lbs/ft is produced. The gear ratio having dropped from 5·4 to 4·0 the push obtained at the driving wheels will now be $\frac{96 \times 4}{1} = 384$ lbs. The push is thus reduced to less than three-quarters of the former figure.

If, instead of changing up at 4,000 r.p.m., we push the engine in third gear, up to its revolution limit of 5,500 r.p.m. where the torque falls to 72 lbs/ft, we will still obtain a push of $\frac{72 \times 5\cdot4}{1} = 389$ lbs.

The revolution limit having been reached we must now change up into top gear, which drops the revolution to about 3,850 r.p.m., where the torque produced is 100 lbs/ft. The overall top gear ratio being 4 : 1, we will obtain a torque at the driving wheels of 400 lbs/ft and a push of 400 lbs. Thus by pushing the engine up to its revolution limit in third gear before changing up into fourth, the push obtained in either gear is constantly being kept at a higher level than the one we can call upon by changing up from third into top as soon as the torque produced by the engine is about to fall off.

In the particular instance we have chosen, the best changing-up speed just about coincided with the maximum permissible engine revolutions. If we had pushed it to even higher revolutions, supposing it could have been done without doing the engine any harm, say to 6,000 r.p.m., there would not have been any benefit. The torque produced by the engine would have fallen to such a low level that, even multiplied by the third gear ratio, it would have been lower than the torque produced in top gear at 3,850 r.p.m., as when changing up from third at 5,500 r.p.m. If you know the torque or power curve of an engine, it is an easy matter to calculate, or better still obtain graphically, the best changing-up speeds. An experienced driver, however, will quickly find these speeds experimentally without any recourse to calculation. As a rule, it may be said that engines of comparatively high specific output, which all produce their peak torque at more than half the revolutions of their peak power, must be extended on all the gears to their revolution limit, if maximum performance is to be obtained. With engines which produce their maximum torque at comparatively low revolutions, say one-third of their peak power revolutions, or even less, it is usually beneficial to change up comparatively early.

Automatic Transmissions

Someone once remarked that automatic gearboxes work extremely well on cars which do not need a gearbox anyway. Originally, there was certainly some truth in this; automatic gearboxes were usually satisfactory only on high-powered and mostly expensive cars. This is probably why so many people found so many good excuses for not buying them. The most common excuse, of course, is that they are much too good drivers to rely on an automatic device for gear changing and much prefer to perform this function themselves. In my experience, this is wrong in about 90% of the cases, where the timing of the gear changes is much better done by an automatic device which also performs the change more smoothly. Moreover, some modern automatic transmissions, and others to come, have a very high efficiency so that they waste hardly any more power and fuel than manual gearboxes. The only real trouble with automatic transmissions is that they cannot think, and have no foresight. All of them are so designed that when a lower gear is in use and the driver releases the accelerator pedal, they immediately shift up into top gear. This also applies to infinitely variable devices. On winding roads and especially on mountain roads, where fast driving calls for bursts of acceleration followed by braking periods, this is most inconvenient, as every time the car comes up to a corner the transmission shifts itself automatically back into top gear. When the accelerator is depressed again, precious time is lost while the engine is being accelerated and the downshift is being executed, while precise control of the power applied to the driving wheels is lost, which can result in sudden, and sometimes dangerous, wheelspin. Thus, if the best results are to be obtained with an automatic transmission, its automaticity must be judiciously controlled by the overriding device with which all the better transmissions are provided, in order to enable the driver to keep a lower gear engaged whenever necessary.

Cars fitted with an automatic transmission do not have a clutch pedal. Only two pedals are left—one for accelerating and one for braking. It seems rather illogical to me to use the right foot *only* to operate both these pedals while leaving the left foot idle. Tests which I have carried out show that merely moving the foot from one pedal to another costs about one-tenth of a second which is added to the driver's reaction time. Braking with the left foot, once it has been mastered, thus increases the safety margin as well as making town driving less jerky by smoothing out the transition from accelerating to braking—of which driving in heavy traffic mainly consists. Unfortunately, while many automatic transmission cars have been designed for easy operation of the brake pedal by the left foot, the dip switch for the headlights has not often been moved from the floor to the steering column—where it should be in such cases, as dipping the headlights and braking are very often called for simultaneously.

Many drivers, of course, will find that their left foot has not been trained to the sensitive control which braking requires. This is merely a matter of habit, which can be readily acquired by practising on a quiet road. Motor-cyclists learn it very quickly because British motor-cycles usually have the brake pedal on the left. The main difficulty seems to face the driver who uses two cars alternately—one with, and one without, a clutch pedal. I personally have never found this to be a great problem, particularly if the two cars are of widely diverse types. It may be different, however, when two otherwise identical cars are driven in quick succession.

Braking

Nothing is destroyed in Nature. The calorific energy contained in the fuel burnt by the engine is transformed into kinetic energy. While the car progresses, this is transformed back into heat generated in the car's various bearings, in the tyres, and by the air drag. All this heat is eventually absorbed by the surrounding

22

air. Braking merely accelerates this process by heating up the brake drums or discs quickly so as to absorb more kinetic energy in a shorter time.

The main problem with braking lies in the fact that the heat generated in the brakes cannot be dissipated into the surrounding air as rapidly as it is produced, so that the brakes quickly become very hot. This discrepancy between the rate of production and absorption of the heat by the surrounding air is increased as the weight of the car and its speed go up for a given drum or disc size. As the size of the brakes cannot be increased in proportion to the weight and the speed of the vehicle, fast driving on winding roads or in heavy traffic, involving frequent use of the brakes, can produce very high temperatures indeed in the brake drums, discs and linings. Temperatures can reach an even higher level when the brakes are used almost continuously, as in the case of a long mountain descent for instance. These high temperatures will produce brake fade, which is mainly due to the decrease of the coefficient of friction between the lining and the metallic drum or disc as the surface temperature exceeds a certain level. Disc brakes, in which heat is generated on a much smaller proportion of the surface at a time, and in which the working surface is directly exposed to the airstream so that the heat does not have to creep through the metal to reach the cooling air, are less prone to fade than drum brakes. In the latter, the reduction in efficiency is accentuated by distortion and by the increase in drum diameter due to expansion, with a consequent increase in the gap between the lining and the drum, thus lengthening the pedal travel and creating a risk of this going down to the floor. It also happens that brakes which have faded badly once, do not recover completely after they have cooled down, as the linings will have lost their original characteristics.

Thus a good driver will never use his brakes more than necessary. He will also remember that two short and quite hard applications of the brakes are better than one long one, as they give the air a chance to circulate between the metal and the lining and to cool them down. This is much more necessary with drum brakes than with disc brakes, in which a large proportion of the working surface is exposed to the cooling air. Of course, the brakes can be saved to quite an appreciable extent by using the engine as a brake, by changing down into a lower gear as soon as the car speed is reduced sufficiently to make this possible without over-revving the engine, and thus relieving them of some part of their work.

It has been said more or less jokingly, that the less a racing driver uses his brakes, the faster he goes. This is of course true in so far as brakes never make a car go, and all unnecessary braking must obviously be avoided. But when a car must, of necessity, be slowed down, very heavy braking indeed is called for if the minimum of time is to be lost. Imagine a car running down a straight at 120 miles an hour towards a bend that can only be taken at 30. Obviously, it will reach the corner quicker if its speed of 120 m.p.h. is held until about 250 yards from the corner, when the driver will have to brake quite heavily in order to make the bend, than if the accelerator is lifted about 1,000 yards before the corner and the car is left to coast towards it relying mainly on the engine and the air drag for slowing down. In the first case, the speed of 120 m.p.h. is held up to the braking point only 250 yards from the corner, whereas in the second case the last 750 yards before the braking point are covered at a steadily decreasing speed. Nevertheless, of two drivers who can go equally fast, the one who uses his brakes less is the better one, and if it comes to an emergency he will be able to go faster than the other by using his brakes harder.

On the ordinary road especially, there is a lot of unnecessary braking which can often be avoided by some foresight, with a consequent saving not only of time but also of fuel, brake linings and tyres. We will go further into this later.

One of the most difficult tasks with which a driver is faced is the judgement of the braking force which should be applied for prevailing road conditions, particularly on slippery surfaces. Except at comparatively slow speeds, the braking distance is increased when a wheel is locked. This means that to achieve the minimum braking distance from high speed, the brakes must be applied hard enough for the wheels to be just on the point of locking without actually doing so. If a wheel does lock, not only is the braking distance increased, but it also loses its ability to guide the vehicle, so that a skid can be induced. Locked front wheels make it impossible for the driver to steer the car, which is a frequent cause of accidents which could have been avoided by more delicate use of the brakes. The usual panic reaction of the average driver to such a situation is to apply the brakes even harder, which of course is anything but helpful. The correct reaction should be to release the pressure on the pedal slightly, in order to give the tyres a chance to re-establish their grip on the road. Admittedly such a reaction calls for quite a lot of practice, and it is not always easy to detect the exact moment when the wheels start turning again.

Drivers who do not think they have the necessary sensitivity can use a slightly less efficient alternative method which leaves a larger margin for error. This consists of applying the brakes quite hard, then releasing the pedal slightly and then again depressing it harder and yet again reducing the pressure on the pedal. This gives the wheels a chance to unlock if the harder application of the brakes has locked them. In most large aircraft, the 'Maxaret' device does just this in very quick succession, which keeps the wheels practically on the locking point while all the pilot has to do is to brake as hard as he can.

Heel-and-Toeing

In order to save as much time as possible it is desirable that, after the car has been slowed down for some reason, maximum acceleration should be available as soon as it is required. This means that the proper gear should have been selected beforehand, so that the driver can call upon the highest available torque at the first touch of the accelerator. This also makes for safer driving as, especially in traffic, a burst of acceleration will save the situation as often as a hard application of the brakes.

When it is important to go fast, any major slowing down involves the use of the brakes. We have already seen that the later the braking point is left, the more time is saved. Moreover, the brakes themselves can be saved by judicious use of the gearbox in order to take advantage of the braking power of the engine. In order to make a correct down-change, without causing a jerk and straining the transmission when the clutch is re-engaged, the engine must be speeded up during the process of the gear change. If the car is being braked at the limit and this precaution is not taken, not only will the transmission be strained, but the driving wheels will tend to lock and may thus initiate a skid. With a non-synchromesh gearbox, not only must the engine be accelerated, but the double de-clutch technique must be used to avoid crashing the gears. If, in order to achieve this, the accelerator pedal is to be depressed in the normal way, it means that the foot must momentarily release the brake pedal in order to actuate the accelerator. The car will thus be left to roll on, unchecked, in the braking area, all the time the brake pedal is left untouched. A jerky progress of the car will result, which may put it off balance, and the braking distance will inevitably be increased. On a fast approach to a slow corner, this increase may be quite significant.

Let us take the example of a fast sports car fitted with a five-speed gearbox, tearing down the straight of the Le Mans circuit at 170 m.p.h. towards Mulsanne Corner, which can be taken at only 40 m.p.h. and for which first gear must be used. If the driver wants to save his brakes to the utmost, he will successively change down into fourth, third, second, and first gear. Four changes—every one of which takes at least half a second—will thus have to be made while the car proceeds unchecked. The average speed of the car while it is being braked from 170 m.p.h. to 40 m.p.h. is 105 m.p.h.; at this speed, 145 feet are covered in every second, so that during the two seconds the car is left unchecked while the four downshifts are performed, it travels 290 feet or just about 100 yards. This distance must, of course, be added to the actual braking distance, so that instead of leaving his braking point until, say, 300 yards before the corner, the driver will have to start braking at 400 yards, thus forsaking another 100 yards of full throttle driving. This is why, with light cars fitted with disc brakes and running in comparatively short races where brake wear is not a problem any more, as is the case with the modern Grand Prix cars, some drivers prefer not to go through all the gears on an approach to a corner, but rather to nip from the gear they were in, directly into the gear required, without going through the intermediates. Even then, however, it is advantageous to use the heel-and-toe method which enables the driver to depress the gas pedal, in order to double de-clutch, without releasing the brakes.

This method consists of actuating the brake pedal with the ball of the foot, which is left to exert its pressure on the pedal, while the heel depresses the accelerator. Alternatively, the brake can be pushed down with the left half of the foot, which is tilted to depress the accelerator with its right half as required (9). The opposite procedure—actuating the brake with the heel and the accelerator with the ball of the foot—is to be avoided at all costs, as the heel is not sufficiently sensitive to give the accuracy necessary for braking under difficult conditions. How far the accelerator is depressed on the other hand is not so important as, with the engine running idle, all that matters is how long the throttle is opened; how far it is opened makes very little difference.

Drivers who have practised this so-called heel-and-toe method of gear changing, will find that they can do it in most cars, and where it does not come easily, the accelerator pedal can in many cases be bent to such an angle that the manœuvre may be performed comfortably.

Not only does heel-and-toeing save time, but it also gives such a sense of safety, due to the fact that the car is kept under the constant control of the driver, that even in ordinary traffic a driver accustomed to using this method finds himself very much at a loss in a car in which he cannot apply it. Passengers also appreciate the smooth progress that results from this drill. It makes starting on hills very much easier too, because the start can be performed without the use of the mostly inefficient and usually inaccessible hand brake.

CHAPTER II

RACING ON ROAD AND TRACK

AS most of the European racing circuits are made up of public roads temporarily closed to traffic, there is no basic difference between such a circuit and a normal road. Only in Britain, where the law forbids the use of public roads for racing, are motor races confined to specially designed tracks, but even these are made to resemble normal roads as closely as possible. What I want to stress in this chapter is that there is a considerable difference between racing on a road that is not intimately known by the driver, and racing on a comparatively short circuit or track on which a certain number of practice laps enable the driver to learn well nigh every inch.

For maximum results, a circuit or a track leaves no room for improvisation. Pre-race practice has enabled the driver to get an almost photographic image of the circuit printed in his mind. He knows exactly what lies behind every blind corner; he knows exactly where to place his car on the road to get the best results; he has progressively found out how fast he can go through any corner and exactly where the limit lies; he has also found out precisely where to brake and where to change gear in order to round any corner or bend, or tackle any other hazard, at the speed practice has proved to be his, and his car's limits.

It follows that the essence of circuit or track racing is the ability of a driver to reach the absolute limits imposed by natural forces upon braking and cornering, to hold his car against these forces, and to repeat the performance on every lap.

Racing on the road, as was best exemplified by the now-defunct Italian Mille Miglia, but which is still to be found in rallies in the form of secret special stages or hill climbs, in the Argentine Road Grand Prix and, in a mitigated form, in the Targa Florio, is a very different sort of racing which calls for a very different sort of ability. Here the driver has no chance of finding where the limit lies by progressive attempts. Every corner, every bend, every hump-back creates a new situation which he must judge rapidly and accurately. But only in a very few cases can he hope to reach the limit allowed by the circumstances; and when he does, he can think himself very lucky not to have exceeded it and to have been able to keep the car on the road. Without knowing the exact shape of the bend or corner that lies before him, not knowing the exact nature of the road surface or its profile, the driver who races on a normal road must, of necessity, allow for any surprise, and keep a slight safety margin in hand. So in contrast with the circuit or track driver, the road driver's art is not to balance his car on the absolute limit of adhesion, but rather to judge as they arise a succession of new situations as accurately as possible, and consistently to reduce the vital safety margin to a minimum. His driving is thus more intuitive than scientific. He must also have a very highly developed sense of observation that will allow him to take advantage of anything that might help him to guess what lies ahead before he actually sees how the road is shaped. Anywhere the road disappears he will look for telegraph poles, trees, road signs, advertising posters, maybe the roof of another car or other things that might give him a clue to the shape of the road ahead. Always keeping in mind the necessity of observing the small safety margin, only occasionally and in an emergency will he have to balance his car on the limit of adhesion, as circuit drivers do on every corner and every time they brake on the approach to it.

It is thus easy to understand why the great road races and hill climbs of motoring history have seldom been won by drivers who became famous by their victories in Grand Prix racing. In the same way, it explains why great road drivers of recent times like Taruffi, Biondetti, Maglioli or Gendebien never reached quite the same heights in Grand Prix racing as in genuine road racing. There is very little reason why one and the same driver should have both the sense of improvisation required of a proper road driver and the sense of balance of a first-class circuit driver; among the greatest drivers of the last thirty years, only Nuvolari and Moss seem to have possessed both attributes at the absolute highest level.

The question who is the greater, a great circuit driver and a great road driver, could be debated for hours. Their specialities are so different that no fair comparison can be drawn between them. However, if I had to answer it, I would probably say that the great road driver is the greater of the two, because his ability is exerted in a less artificial sphere than circuit or track racing. His ability calls for constantly taking new decisions which must of necessity be right, otherwise he will lose time or go off the road, whereas pre-race practice enables the circuit or track driver to try for the limit progressively, as often as he likes, without taking great risks. On the other hand, circuit or track driving is a more scientific approach to driving than open road racing. Here the driver knows most of the factors of the problem to be solved, which is usually to take a bend or a succession of bends, including the braking area on the approach to them, as quickly as possible. If all the factors were known with complete precision, the quickest way through any particular portion of a circuit or track could actually be calculated. I do not think that anybody has ever actually done it, but the basic principles of how to get the best results have been laid down and confirmed in actual practice. In fact, theory has only proved what had been found out long ago by plain common sense and practical experience.

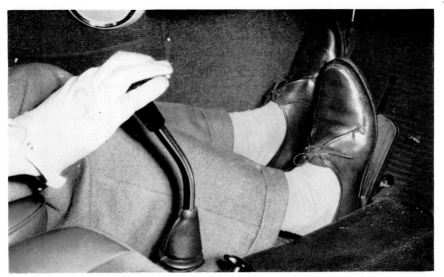

9 'Heel-and-toe' is perhaps not an entirely correct description of how to operate the brake and accelerator pedal of a modern car while double-declutching and simultaneously braking into a corner. The required dab on the accelerator is more usually given by tilting the foot without releasing its pressure on the brake

10 Having prepared for the corner, Stirling Moss turns the wheel to full lock in a single smooth movement to take the Station hairpin in the 1961 Monte Carlo Grand Prix, which he won

11 Richie Ginther (Ferrari), Graham Hill (B.R.M.) and Jim Clark (Lotus) take three different lines into a 180-degree bend. Ginther's is the 'textbook line' while Clark adopts the 'Moss Line', cutting in close right from the start of the corner. Ginther's line results in a slightly increased radius in the second half of the bend, and thus a slightly higher exit speed, while Clark's line is shorter and permits slightly later braking. In fact the various lines were probably chosen by the drivers in accordance with the handling characteristics of their respective cars: the strongly understeering front-engined Ferrari wants to be turned into the corner on the overrun and accelerated whilst its course is straightened, while the Lotus driver will manage to drive his car round the bend under power without excessive understeer

12 The author, driving a Ferrari in the 1955 Belgian Grand Prix, demonstrates how to cut a hairpin bend well beyond its apex, in order to straighten the line at the exit and accelerate the car quicker into the following straight

CHAPTER III

CORNERING

IN this chapter we will try to lay down the main principles of cornering, based on the natural forces acting upon a car when the direction of its movement is changed. The ability of a car to be steered derives from the adhesion of its tyres on the road. This adhesion is ruled by the coefficient of adhesion which varies with the state and the nature of the road surface and is directly related to the weight of the car. This relationship is given by the formula:

$$A = W \times E,$$

W being the car's weight and E the coefficient of adhesion.

Under good conditions, E lies at around $0 \cdot 8$. This means that if we want to push a car weighing 2,000 lbs sideways, a push of 1,600 lbs will be required. If all wheels are locked, the same push will be required to move the car forward or in any other horizontal direction. As long as a car rolls forward in a straight line, its adhesion, which enables it to resist lateral or sideways forces, remains intact. As soon as it is being braked or driven, or as it changes direction, inertia forces are created which use up part of the available adhesion.

Let us first take the case of a car that has already been driven from a straight line into a bend, and which now rounds it following a constant radius and at a constant speed. In this condition, the car is submitted to a centrifugal force:

$$F_c = \frac{m \times v^2}{R},$$

m being the mass of the car, v its velocity and R the radius of the curve.

This force is directed along the line going from the centre of the curve to the centre of gravity of the car. It can be broken down into two components, one acting rearward along the centre

33

line of the car, the other perpendicular to it and very nearly equal in force and direction to the centrifugal force itself as long as the curve is of comparatively large radius.

The centrifugal force being proportional to the mass of the car and thus to its weight $\left(\text{the mass being } m = \dfrac{\text{weight}}{\text{gravity}}\right)$, it is also proportional to the vehicle's adhesion. Thus the lighter the car, the smaller the centrifugal force, which shows that the often-expressed opinion that light cars are more dangerous than heavy ones, because they are more prone to slide, is entirely false.

Of much greater interest are the two facts that the centrifugal force is proportional to the square of the speed and inversely proportional to the radius of the curve. The limit of adhesion at which the car will start to slide being reached when the main component of the centrifugal force (the one that acts at a right angle to the car's centre line) becomes equal to the vehicle's adhesion, we find that by making the fullest use of the width of the road to increase the radius of the curve along which the vehicle travels, the centrifugal force will be reduced for a given speed of the car. A greater safety margin is thus provided, and the speed can be increased further before the limit is reached. This is what is done in racing. The line of greatest radius that can be inscribed into a given curved section of road starts as close as possible to the verge of the road that lies on the outside of the corner, closes in towards the inside so as to put the car nearest the inside verge at the apex of the corner, then goes out again to the outside which is reached tangentially, when the car is straightened (*13*). In the

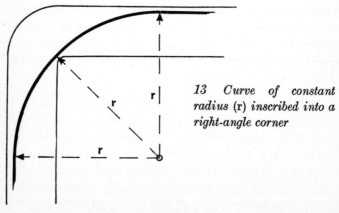

13   Curve   of   constant radius (r) *inscribed into a right-angle corner*

34

case of a perfectly regular bend, the point where the car comes closest to the inside verge lies exactly half-way through the corner. This, theoretically, is the fastest way through a corner, not taking into account the phases of entering the corner and leaving it which will be discussed later.

The aim of a racing driver, however, is not to drive as quickly as possible round any given corner or bend, but to lap a given circuit as fast as possible. Surprising as it may sound, this means that the bends and corners included in the circuit will have to be taken slightly slower than the absolute maximum they allow. This is because every bend and corner must be considered in conjunction with the straight, or straighter portion of road, into which it leads. Every circuit is made up of bends, corners and faster stretches on which the car accelerates until it must be checked again for the next hazard. A straight is seldom long enough for the car to reach its absolute maximum speed; the progression of the racing car is thus mainly made up of bursts of acceleration followed by braking. If, to simplify the issue, we assume that the acceleration of a car along a straight is constant until the driver has to apply the brakes again, it is obvious that the faster the car comes into the straight, the faster will be its average speed along this straight up to the next braking point. For example, if one driver goes into the straight at 60 m.p.h., and accelerates to 120 m.p.h. before he must brake again, a better driver who has gone into the straight at 65 m.p.h., driving an identical car, will have reached 125 m.p.h. before he comes to the end of the straight. In the first instance, the average speed along the straight will have been 90 m.p.h., in the second 95 m.p.h. This is, in fact, not quite true in practice, as the rate of acceleration of a car decreases as its speed increases, but it shows that if the straight is long enough, the gain thus achieved may warrant a slightly slower average speed around the bend that precedes it, if this enables the driver to leave the bend at a higher speed and thus get a better run into the straight.

We have seen previously that the highest constant speed round a bend is reached by taking the line corresponding to the greatest radius that can be inscribed into the particular portion of road in question. For a given radius and coefficient of adhesion of the road, there is a corresponding speed that cannot be exceeded if the car is not to be pulled off the road by the centrifugal force. This in turn means that if the car is being driven round a corner at the maximum permissible speed, it cannot be accelerated until it has reached the end of the bend. In order to reach the straight at a speed higher than the maximum speed compatible with the corner, we must adopt a line that is different from the one resulting in the highest speed through the bend itself. This new line follows a curve of variable radius; at the beginning of the bend, the new line will be more sharply curved than the original line of constant radius that enables the curve itself to be taken at the highest possible speed; in the second part of the curve it will then progressively straighten up to a curve of longer radius than the original regular arc (*14*).

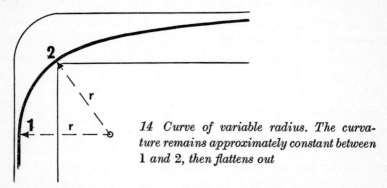

14 Curve of variable radius. The curvature remains approximately constant between 1 and 2, then flattens out

Due to the sharper curve of the new line followed by the car in the first part of the bend, its speed will have to be reduced to a slightly lower figure than the one allowed by the original line of constant curvature. As soon, however, as it reaches the point where the curve starts to widen, the car can be accelerated as the progressive decrease of the curvature allows a progressive increase in its speed. The vehicle can thus be accelerated before it reaches the end of the curve, and the point before which it was not previously possible to accelerate along the line of constant curvature will be reached at a higher speed, thus giving a faster run into the following straight.

The advantage which results from using this method is quite easy to understand. Let us suppose that it takes the car about 2 seconds to round the bend and that it spends about 10 seconds on the straight before it must be slowed for the next bend: it thus spends five times as long on the straight as it does in the bend. If the line of variable radius taken through the bend costs 2 m.p.h. in average speed through the bend, but makes possible an increase of 2 m.p.h. in the average speed of the car along the straight, there will be a saving in time along the straight five times greater than what has been lost around the bend.

It will be seen that, instead of cutting the corner at its apex (that is, exactly half-way round the bend when this is of constant

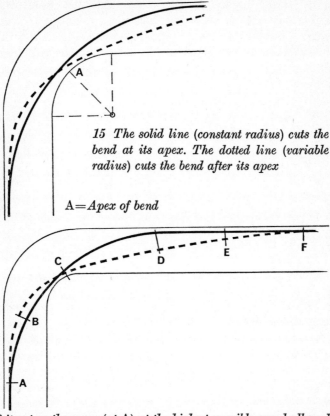

15 The solid line (constant radius) cuts the bend at its apex. The dotted line (variable radius) cuts the bend after its apex

A=*Apex of bend*

16 If it enters the curve (at A) at the highest possible speed allowed by its adhesion, a car that follows the line of constant radius (solid line) cannot exceed this speed until the end of the curve is reached (at D). A car that follows the dotted line of variable radius must slow more to enter the corner, because its curvature is more accentuated. If the curve can be taken at 80 m.p.h. along the solid line, the speed of a car following the dotted line will be less at B (say 78 m.p.h.). But from C on, the car following this line can be accelerated. At D, its speed may already have reached 85 m.p.h., when the car following the solid line is only just finishing its constant curve at 80 m.p.h. and can only now be accelerated. At E and F, and all along the following stretch, the car on the dotted line will be the faster

37

curvature), this new corrected line brings the car closest to the inside of the road at a slightly later moment (*15*). This closest point is moved along the corner towards its exit as the irregularity of the curvature of the line taken by the car is increased. Just how much the actual line to be taken should deviate from the ideal line of the greatest constant radius that can be inscribed into the particular portion of road under consideration, entirely depends on the performance of the car. If it has only just enough power to move it along the curve at the highest speed at which the bend can be taken, but cannot be accelerated any further, the ideal line of constant radius is the obvious choice. If, on the other hand, the car is capable of very high acceleration, it will be advantageous to increase the curvature of the line quite considerably upon entering the bend, in order to be able to straighten it in the second half of the curve so as to make full use of the car's acceleration (*16*). For a car with a performance between these two extremes, an intermediate line will give the best results. The benefit of taking a line of markedly variable curvature is particularly obvious on hairpin bends, which are taken by most fast cars in first gear, on which the acceleration is usually very quick (*12*).

This technique however can also be overdone, and in many competition driving courses too much emphasis is put upon the necessity of increasing the curvature of the line into a corner, the better to straighten it coming out of the corner, so that drivers end up taking the bend before they actually get into it. They describe a curve that is much sharper than necessary, and then drive through the corner in a nearly straight line.

If a car is to round a corner as quickly as possible, it must, from the moment it is turned into the corner to the moment its course is straightened again, be kept at the limit of adhesion. This means that the line it follows in the second part of the corner must only be opened up as much as the increasing speed of the car makes this necessary to keep it just below the limit of adhesion. If, in the second part of the corner, the course is straightened to the extent that full use is not made of the available adhesion, then time has been lost in entering the bend along a line of shorter radius than is necessary.

Driving Into and Out of a Corner

Up to now we have considered a car in the process of taking a curve of approximately constant radius and at approximately constant speed. We have neglected the inertia forces which take charge when the car is turned from a straight into a corner, or from a corner into a straight, and also every time the radius of the curve described by the car or the speed of the latter are varied. When a vehicle describes a curve, it not only rolls along a curved line, but also turns around its own vertical axis. A car running in a straight line has a rotational speed of zero around its vertical axis; when it rounds a turn of constant radius and at a constant speed, it has a uniform rotational speed and, but for frictional losses, would not need any outside force to maintain it. The car having a certain inertia around its own vertical axis however, a force is needed to produce the rotating movement when it is being driven from a straight into a curve. Conversely, a force of opposite direction will be needed to stop the rotating movement when the car comes out of the turn and into the straight again. The best demonstration of the sort of forces involved can be made when a car is hoisted on a single-column lift in a service station. These lifts can turn round their own vertical axis which usually more or less coincides with the vertical axis going through the centre of gravity of the car that is hoisted on them. If you try to turn the lift round you will find that quite a considerable force is needed to start it moving, but that once it turns, the force necessary to keep it on the move is quite small, as it is only necessary to compensate for the friction in the lifting mechanism. The greater force required to start the movement is needed to counteract the inertia of the car; for a given leverage around the axis of the lift, the force it is necessary to apply is proportional to the rate at which the rotational speed of the vehicle is to be accelerated. Neglecting the friction in the mechanism, an equal force resulting in an equal torque around the lift's vertical axis (which we assume coincides with the vertical axis going through the centre of gravity of the car) must be exerted in the opposite direction if the rotation is to be stopped at an equivalent rate of deceleration (17).

When a car is being driven from a straight line into a turn, a torque must be applied round the vertical axis going through its centre of gravity in order to start it turning against its own inertia. This torque is created by forces acting through the contact points of the wheels with the road surface. Due to its inertia, the car reacts in the opposite direction so that at the start of a corner, and as long as the radius of the curve into which the car is turned

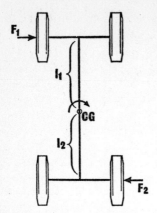

17 To start a vehicle turning around its own vertical axis, a force must be exerted at the front and rear axles to create a torque $F_1l_1 + F_2l_2$. The wheels will react on the ground with equal forces but in the opposite direction. These forces are proportional to the moment of inertia of the car around the vertical axis going through the centre of gravity and they increase as the square of the acceleration of the rotational movement

18 When a car starts a turn, the lateral component F_l of the centrifugal force F_c acts in the same direction as the reaction force F_{r1} created by the car's moment of inertia at the front axle and in the opposite direction to the reaction force F_{r2} created at the rear axle, thus tending to create a front-wheel slide

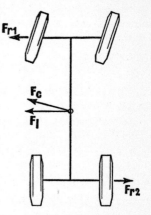

decreases, the reaction tends to pull the front wheels outwards and the rear wheels inwards. The reaction upon the front wheels being in approximately the same direction as the centrifugal force, if a car is turned too brutally into a corner this reaction, plus the component of the centrifugal force acting upon the front wheels, can add up to a total exceeding the adhesion of the front wheels which may start a front-wheel slide (*18*). At the end of the bend, when the course of the car is being straightened up again, forces and reaction forces are reversed to stop the rotation of the car around its own vertical axis. The reaction upon the front wheels now tends to pull them inwards against the centrifugal force, whereas the reaction upon the rear wheels tends to pull them outwards and thus is added to the component of the centrifugal force acting upon the rear wheels. Thus, if the course is straightened up too sharply following a curve which has been taken near the limit of adhesion, a rear-wheel slide can be induced.

On account of this rotational inertia, the car must of necessity

19 This Austin-Healey failed to cut the bend close enough and went spinning out of control when the driver tried to force it around along a too sharply curved line

20 With cars running in close company, it is not always possible, or even desirable, to take the academic line through a bend. Here Willy Mairesse took what was probably the most desirable line into a 180-degree turn, but Luciano Bianchi has managed to nip into the inside and might just be able to force the leading car out of its line at the exit. Had Mairesse kept closer in he might have lost a few hundredths of a second, but he could not have been pushed off his line and would have been certain to stay in front

21 *Olivier Gendebien's Ferrari on the banking at Montlhéry. Close observation of the picture will show that the suspension is about fully compressed by the centrifugal force pushing the car down on the track*

22 *The author instructing a Porsche driver in a competition driving course to cut into the gutter with the inside front wheel, in order to shorten the curve and to create a banking effect as the car leans into the lower level of the gutter*

be driven progressively into the curve and out of it, which in turn means that the line of the greatest radius that can be inscribed into the bend considered, cannot start and finish at the extreme outside verges of the road, as originally suggested. This also applies to the alternative modified line suggested, starting with a slightly sharper curve that is progressively straightened up in the second part of the bend. In both cases, the car must be steered progressively, but as quickly as possible by a rather sharp movement of the steering wheel, into the curve which takes it off the extreme verge of the road until the line of proper curvature has been reached, and then led back again progressively into the straight.

Transitory Turn

In fact there is a way of progressively driving the car into the turn, without leaving the extreme verge of the road before the car is following the line of proper curvature. Many drivers adopt it without actually realising it, simply because they do not like driving for any long distance, only a few inches away from the verge of the road, until they get to a corner. As a result, on the approach to the corner, they drive obliquely towards the outside verge, aiming their car at the point where it must be turned into the bend on to the line of proper curvature. In order to clear the verge towards which the car is driven, the turn must be started a little earlier than if the car were being driven parallel to the verge, thus making it possible for the driver to turn his car progressively on to the line of

23   The transitory turn (from A to B) leads the car progressively into the main curve

proper curvature, which is initiated at the exact point where the sweep comes nearest to the outside edge of the road—and thus without wasting any space (*23*).

If he is determined to go really fast, an experienced driver approaching an unknown, fast corner which he cannot entirely

43

overlook, will automatically find himself flicking the steering wheel to and fro in a quick succession of rather small movements. His aim—though, as they do it instinctively, very few drivers realise it—is to impart the car with an oscillating, snaking movement of small amplitude, but sufficient to start it turning to one side, then the other, so that it will turn more readily into the bend when the driver thinks fit to do so. In fact, the driver puts his car in a succession of small transitory curves, of which he picks the one that seems most suitable for turning the car into the bend.

Succession of Bends

In accordance with the principle that it is more important for the car to leave a bend or a corner accelerating early and fast, than to round it at the maximum speed, a succession of bends in opposite directions, following one another at too short intervals for the car to be placed correctly for each one to be taken individually, must be tackled in such a way that the car is correctly placed for the last bend to be taken at the highest possible speed. This will give the car the best run into the following straight. This means that the bend *before* the last must be taken in such a way that the car leaves it not on the outside but near the inside of the road so that it is placed correctly to take the last bend under the best possible conditions. The speed through the penultimate bend is thus sacrificed to the line through the last of the series. Through the previous bends, the line must, of course, be a compromise between making full use of the width of the road at the exit of one corner and placing the car correctly for the next one. The line to be followed depends solely upon the distance to the next bend in the opposite direction and the opportunity afforded to reposition the car correctly for it. A good driver always takes a perfectly smooth and flowing line along any piece of road—never an angular one.

Taking Advantage of the Road Camber (see Appendix)

Up to now, we have been assuming that the road was a perfectly flat and level surface. This is usually true only of aerodrome circuits. Ordinary roads are normally slightly domed, in order to allow water to drain away, so that the inside of bends is inclined inwards, forming a sort of banking, and on modern, properly engineered highways, bends are banked on their entire width.

Such a banking allows a considerable increase of the car's

speed through the bend, as figures 24 and 25 will show. In order to simplify matters, we will assume that the vehicle is driven on a road surface giving exceptional grip, equivalent to a coefficient of adhesion=1. This means that the adhesion of the car on a level road is equal to its weight W.

Let us first assume the car to be stopped on the banking, when the weight W can be broken up into a lateral force, parallel to the plane of the road, F_{lw}, and a force parallel to the vertical axis of the car (i.e. perpendicular to the road surface) F_{vw} (see figs. 59 and 60 of Appendix). This force F_{vw} being less than W, it follows that the inclination of the road reduces the adhesion of the vehicle by the amount $W-F_{vw}$. On the other hand, the lateral component tends to pull the car down the banking and will actually succeed in doing so if the angle of the banking reaches 45 degrees (or less if the coefficience of adhesion were less than 1, which it usually is).

If the car is now set moving round the bend, another set of forces will be created, originated by the centrifugal force F_c. This can again be broken up into a lateral force F_{lc}, acting parallel to the road surface, and a force parallel to the vertical axis of the car (i.e. perpendicular to the road surface) F_{vc}. The steeper the banking, the smaller the lateral force F_{lc} becomes for a given centrifugal force F_c, and the greater becomes the component F_{vc} which increases the adhesion of the car on the road.

In competition driving, we are interested only in fast cornering giving rise to high centrifugal forces, in which case:

(a) F_{vc} is always greater than $W-F_{vw}$, which means that the adhesion of the car on the road is increased, enabling it to be cornered faster.

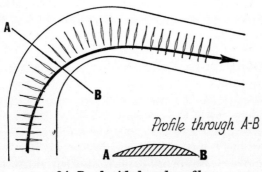

Profile through A-B

24 Road with domed profile

(b) F_{lc} is not only smaller than the centrifugal force F_c itself, but is counteracted by F_{lw}, so that the resultant force tending to pull the vehicle outward is considerably less than the centrifugal force which would act upon the car on an unbanked corner.

The overall result is that, on a banked corner, the increased adhesion and—for a given speed—reduced lateral force allow the car to be driven considerably faster round a bend of a given radius,

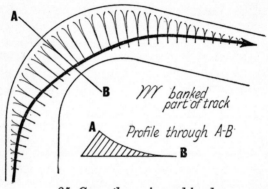

25 *Correctly engineered bend*

even if the banking angle is only a few degrees. The driver must naturally try to take full advantage of this and eventually choose his line accordingly.

If, for instance, the road has a domed profile, resulting in an adverse camber on the outside of the bend, of which the adverse effect upon the adhesion of the vehicle is as marked as the correct camber is beneficial, the extreme outside of the bend must be avoided at all costs and the road must be treated as if it were narrower than it actually is. Moreover, the curve of the line taken through the bend must be adapted to the change of the banking angle, first being increased as the car gets nearer to the inner verge, then decreased as, beyond the apex of the bend, it is driven back towards the centre of the road (*24*).

The profile of a correctly engineered bend, featuring a steeper banking angle at the outside of the bend than on the inside calls for an entirely different technique. In this case, the sharpest turns are taken at the beginning and at the end of the bend, when the car is nearest the outside verge where the banking angle is steepest, while the curve is straightened when the car reaches the inside of the bend, where the road is flattest (*25*).

It is sometimes difficult for drivers without racing experience to appreciate how important it is to look out for any variation in the banking of the road and take advantage of it, but icy conditions vividly illustrate this, when, on a slightly domed road, the car can be taken round a curve, along the inner verge, at a speed which would be quite impossible if it were driven on the crown of the road (*22*).

So far, we have dealt only with slightly banked curves, as are found on normal roads or road racing circuits. The long and steep banked curves, usually forming a complete semi-circle, used to connect the two straights of a racing or test track, such as those at Montlhéry, Monza, Avus or M.I.R.A., call for an entirely different technique. On a track of this description, only a very slight increase of the radius of the curve described by the car can be gained by the usual cornering technique of entering the curve wide, cutting it at its apex and leaving it wide again, while cutting it at its apex implies that the car must be driven over an almost horizontal part of the track, instead of making use of the banking all the way round the curve.

On a properly designed banking, a car can be driven at any speed without being subjected to any lateral force tending to make it slide and deviate from its line. In order to achieve this, the driver must hold it on a line where, at the particular speed adopted, the angle of the banking is such that the lateral components F_{lw} and F_{cw} created by the weight of the vehicle and by the centrifugal force respectively, cancel each other out (*60*). This line is not only the safest, as it rules out any possibility of a slide, but is also the fastest, as it eliminates all power-absorbing side thrust on the tyres, though with slow cars, which must be kept on a low line on the banking, the fastest line may sometimes lie somewhere between the no side-thrust line and the shortest round the curve, i.e. its extreme inside.

Owing to the fact that a car subjected to a sideways force tends to deviate in the direction of this force, it is very easy for the driver to find the line on the banking along which, at the speed reached by his car, all sideways forces cancel each other out. He must hold the steering wheel very lightly and let the car settle where it is pulled neither outwards by centrifugal action, nor inwards by gravity. In other words, the car must be left to find the

47

correct line itself. All the driver has to do then is to drive it from the straight into the banked curve along a line corresponding to the correct position of the car on the banking, so that it will not have to be driven up or pulled down, once it is in the curve.

As on a banked track the faster cars must be driven higher up the banking, slower cars must be overtaken from above, which means that, where the cars run anti-clockwise, the normal rule of the track is reversed and overtaking cars must pass slower vehicles on the right.

If, on a properly designed banked track, lateral forces tending to pull the car off its line can be entirely cancelled out, another difficulty arises at high speed. This is due to the component of the centrifugal force F_{vc} acting perpendicularly to the track. It increases the force with which the vehicle bears upon the road, and is equivalent—as far as the strain put on the tyres, the wheels, the suspension and the chassis frame is concerned—to an increase in the weight of the vehicle (21).

It can be calculated that, when the lateral forces cancel out on a curve with a banking of 45 degrees (i.e. when the centrifugal force is equal to the weight of the car), the total force with which the car bears upon the road is about 1·4 times its own weight. This condition is reached, for a curve of 250 metres (650 feet) radius, at a speed of 178 k.p.h. (110 m.p.h.). If, for the lateral forces to cancel out, the car must be driven higher up the banking, the force pushing it down on the road is notably increased. For a centrifugal force equal to twice the weight of the car, a banking angle of 64 degrees is required and the force with which the car bears upon the road is increased to as much as 2·25 times its own weight. For a curve of 250 metres (760 feet) radius, this condition is reached at a speed of 252 k.p.h. (157 m.p.h.). (See Appendix.)

For this reason drivers and manufacturers should never agree to race fast cars, which have not been specifically designed for this sort of racing, on banked tracks where the 'natural' line (i.e. the line along which the car steers itself automatically) taken by the car at the highest speed it reaches on the banking corresponds to an inclination of more than 45 degrees. Modern racing-car chassis are built to a very low weight limit and cannot be expected to take more than 50% overstressing without risk of failure—and the kind of failure that may be expected is most likely to be highly dangerous for the driver, other competitors, and even the public surrounding the track.

CHAPTER IV

FROM SLIPPING TO SLIDING

Slipping

IF a wheel and tyre are allowed to roll without any lateral force acting upon them, they will roll in a straight line that lies in the plane of the wheel. Any force acting at a right angle to the plane of the rolling wheel will deflect it in the direction of the force applied. If this force is less than the adhesion of the wheel on the road, there will be no sliding of the tyre on the road; the deviation will be due entirely to the deformation of the tyre. This deviation, which is proportional to the sideways force acting upon the wheel and tyre, is called the 'slip', as opposed to a slide which takes place when the limit of adhesion has been exceeded. The angle included between the plane of the wheel and the path it follows under the action of the sideways force acting upon it, is called the slip angle. The deviation is caused by the lateral deflection of the tyre under the force that pushes it sideways. Due to this deflection, the path of the tread of the rolling tyre that is not in contact with the ground is not in line with the centre of the contact surface; it is deviated some distance in the direction of the force acting upon the wheel (*26*). When some part of that free tread comes into contact with the ground, the centre of its contact surface will thus not be in the same alignment as the centre of the contact surface previously considered. A good idea of what actually happens can be obtained by rolling a circular indiarubber, such as is used for typewriting, on a table and at the same time pushing it laterally while it is held down firmly enough on the table to prevent skidding.

Thus under the influence of a lateral force, such as is produced by the centrifugal force acting upon a car, a rolling wheel and tyre will deviate from its plane, without actually sliding. As a result, even without skidding and at comparatively low speed, a car rounding a corner will not follow the exact path indicated by the

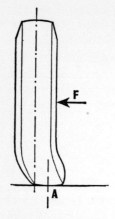

26 When a force F is applied at a right angle to the plane of the wheel, the tyre deflects and the centre A of its contact surface with the road is not in line with the wheel's vertical plane of symmetry

geometry of its wheels (*27*). The actual geometry of the turn will be given by the actual path followed by the wheels, taking into account their slip angle. Any increase or decrease of the slip angle will modify the path followed by the vehicle, having the same effect as a modification to the orientation of the wheels. This form of steering is of course done by the rear wheels as well as by the front wheels of the vehicle. For a given tyre, the slip angle is mainly dependent upon four factors:

(*a*) The sideways force acting upon the wheel. Any increase of this force will obviously increase the slip angle.

(*b*) The tyre pressure. Any increase of the pressure in the tyre will decrease its lateral flexibility and thus reduce the slip angle; conversely, any decrease in the pressure will augment it.

27 Plan view of rolling wheel submitted to a force F applied at a right angle to its plane (lateral force). The centre of the contact point of the tyre with the road (A) is offset to the side and to the rear. The angle α is the slip angle. Instead of following the direction of its own plane, the wheel is deviated along the line AB

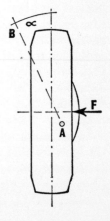

(c) The weight carried by the tyre. For a given lateral force, the slip angle of a tyre is at its minimum around the weight for which the tyre has been designed. Increasing or decreasing the weight by any considerable amount will augment the slip angle.

(d) The camber of the wheel. Positive camber of the wheels increases the slip angle under given conditions, whereas, up to a certain limit, negative camber reduces it.

Sliding

The slip angle reaches a maximum when the lateral force acting upon the wheel approaches the latter's adhesion on the ground. When the adhesion is exceeded, the slip is turned into a slide, when the tyre actually scrubs over the road. Obviously the angle of slide is added to the angle of slip.

Whereas slipping can only be provoked by a force acting in a perpendicular direction to the plane of the wheel, sliding can also be induced by forces acting in the same plane as the wheel, that is, by braking or driving forces.

The adhesion of the tyre on the road is the same in all directions. This means that if we want to pull a locked wheel in its own plane, we will have to exert the same force as is needed to move it sideways or in any other direction. Similarly, if torque is applied to the wheel, the driving force acting upon the ground cannot exceed the adhesion of the wheel.

The important fact in this connection is that any amount of adhesion used up by a driving or braking force reduces the resistance with which the wheel can oppose a force acting perpendicularly to its plane. The constancy of the adhesion in all directions can be represented diagrammatically by a circle which has its centre at the contact point of the tyre with the road (28). The radius of this circle gives the measure of the force of adhesion. If a force greater than the radius of the circle is applied in any direction at the contact point of the tyre with the road, the tyre will slide; if the force applied is less than the radius of the circle, it will not move. All forces applied to the contact point (for the sake of simplicity we will consider that the contact patch between the tyre and the road surface is a point) can be broken down into (1) a force acting perpendicularly to the plane of the wheel and (2) a force acting in the plane of the latter. These two forces are interdependent; if a force less than the adhesion force is applied in

51

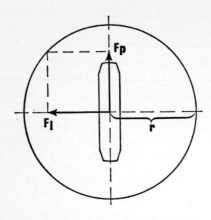

28 r is the measure of the tyre's adhesion on the road. If a force F_l acts laterally upon the wheel, F_p remains available to propel the vehicle or, conversely, for braking. If a driving or braking force F_p is applied, any lateral force greater than F_l will produce a slide. F_l is thus the maximum 'total adhesion' available against sliding when a driving or braking force F_p is applied through the contact surface of the tyre with the road. Total adhesion$=\sqrt{F_p{}^2+F_l{}^2}$

the plane of the wheel (that is, a driving or a braking force) the resistance opposed by the tyre to a force acting perpendicularly to the plane of the wheel (that is, to a force that tends to make it slide sideways) will be reduced. Conversely, any force acting at a right angle to the wheel plane (that is, a force that tends to make the car slide) will reduce its driving or braking power. These forces are related by the formula:

$$\text{Total Adhesion}=\sqrt{F_p{}^2+F_l{}^2},$$

F_p being the force acting in the plane of the wheel and F_l the lateral force.

Thus, if a force F_p is put through the wheel to drive or brake the vehicle, a force F_l acting at right angles to the plane of the wheel $F_l=\sqrt{(\text{Total Adhesion})^2-F_p{}^2}$ will suffice to make the wheel slide. Consequently, if the wheel is submitted to a sideways force F_l, the maximum driving force it will be able to transmit without spinning will be $F_p=\sqrt{(\text{Total Adhesion})^2-F_l{}^2}$.

This formula shows not only that any force applied in one of the planes reduces the ability of the wheel to resist forces in the plane acting at right angles to the force applied, but also that if one of the forces is equal to the adhesion of the tyre on the road, there will be no adhesion left to oppose any other force This means that if a wheel is spinning under an excessive driving torque or is locked in braking, it will not be able to resist skidding in any way; conversely, if the wheel is skidding, with no driving or braking force applied, it will not be able to transmit either of these if required. This explains why even an ordinary touring car that is being cornered steadily on a slippery road under a small throttle opening, will slide as soon as the throttle is opened wide enough in an intermediate gear to make the driving wheels spin. The power slide thus produced will stop only if the throttle is released enough to reduce the driving force to an amount compatible with the lateral force acting upon the wheel, or if the car is steered straight out of the corner so as to reduce the lateral force acting upon the wheel to a value compatible with the driving force applied. These are in fact the two means by which the driver can correct a skid.

Oversteer and Understeer

The exact point where, under the influence of an increasing lateral force acting upon a rolling wheel, the slide takes over from the slip, is very difficult to assess. The practical effect of either of them, however, is that the wheel rolls at an angle to its own plane. Consequently, they have a very similar bearing upon the attitude of the car, changing its direction of travel independently of the driver's action upon the steering. When, under a certain lateral force, the slip angle of the front wheels is smaller than the slip angle of the rear wheels, the vehicle is said to oversteer because it actually makes a tighter turn than the one corresponding to the geometrical position of the wheels (*29*). If the slip angle of the front wheels is greater than that of the rear wheels, the car understeers; it takes a wider turn than the one corresponding to the geometrical position of the wheels (*30*). Equal slip angles front and rear will result in a so-called neutral-steer car. In practice, a neutral-steer car, that is, a car rounding a bend with equal slip angles front and rear, will not exactly follow the line dictated by the geometrical position of its wheels, but will describe a circle of larger radius. It would follow the geometrically defined circle only if the slip angles were nil, or if the car oversteered very slightly.

The ratio of front to rear slip angle varies not only according to the car under consideration but even for one and the same car under differing conditions. Many cars behave differently according to the lateral force acting upon them and some are actually designed to do so. This is mostly achieved by using front and rear suspensions of different geometries, so that when the car leans to one side under the effect of a lateral force acting upon its centre of

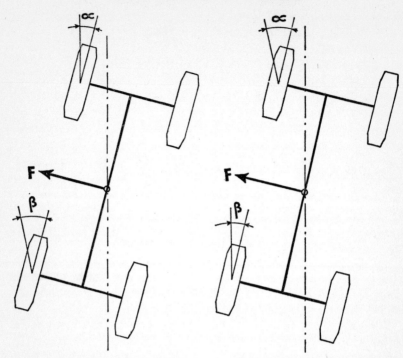

29 *Oversteering car* $\alpha < \beta$. *The front slip angle is narrower than the rear slip angle. The vehicle tends to deviate farther from its original line of progress*

30 *Understeering car* $\alpha > \beta$. *The front slip angle is greater than the rear slip angle. The vehicle, deviated from its line, tends to turn back to its original direction of progress*

gravity, the camber and the orientation of the front and rear wheels follow different patterns.

But even if one wished to design a car possessing absolutely constant cornering characteristics, for example a car that would remain neutral whatever the lateral force acting upon it, it would be impossible to do so. The reason for this is that, under various circumstances, the forces acting at a right angle to the plane of the front and rear wheels respectively, do not always keep the same proportions. When it is being turned into a corner, a car will tend to understeer due to its own inertia; the quicker it is turned into it, the more will it do so. When the car is turned straight again, the inertia forces are reversed which will tend to make it oversteer.

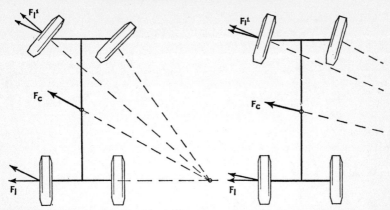

31 As the radius of the turn decreases, the lateral component F_l of the centrifugal force F_c acting upon the rear wheels decreases more than the component F_l^1 acting upon the front wheels

This is hardly noticeable to the driver, however, as at the same time, the centrifugal force is being reduced, thus lessening the lateral thrust upon the tyres and reducing their slip angles.

For any given value of the centrifugal force, the component acting at a right angle to the rear wheels decreases more than the component acting upon the front wheels, as the radius of the

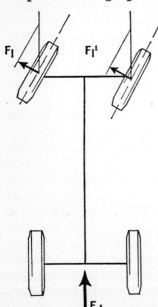

32 In a rear-wheel-drive car, the driving force F_d creates a lateral component force (F_l and F_l^1) acting upon the front wheels as these are turned into a curve

corner decreases (*31*). Thus the sharper the corner, the less oversteer will be noticed and the more understeer will become apparent.

On a rear-wheel-drive car, the driving force is always exerted by the rear axle along the longitudinal axis of the vehicle. As the front wheels are turned, the driving force creates a lateral component upon the front wheels which becomes greater as the lock of the front wheels is increased (*32*). This obviously creates an additional degree of understeer which is added to the normal tendency of an understeering car, or can even momentarily induce a basically oversteering car to understeer.

Turning Understeer into Oversteer

An understeering car is a stable car whereas an oversteering car progresses in an unbalanced state. This is easy to understand: as soon as a car is deviated from its straight line of progress, a centrifugal force is created which acts upon the car and causes the tyres to slip. The slip angle at the front wheels of an understeering car being greater than the slip angle at the rear wheels, the car will automatically tend to turn back to its original direction of progress. If, however, the car oversteers, due to the slip angle at the rear wheels being greater than the slip angle at the front wheels, the car will steer itself towards the direction into which it has been deviated, thus accentuating the deviation. This in turn will increase the centrifugal force acting upon it, the front and rear slip angle differential will be increased, and if the driver does not take immediate action, the car will turn into an increasingly sharper curve and eventually spin. Slight oversteer, however, is not necessarily a disadvantage provided the driver has the ability to control it properly; it helps the vehicle to turn from a straight line into a corner and increases its agility on winding roads where an understeering car that tends to straighten itself automatically will be at a disadvantage.

Another advantage of an oversteering car is derived from its different attitude as it rounds a bend. Due to the fact that the slip angle at the rear wheels is greater than the slip angle at the front wheels, when it leaves a bend the car becomes aligned with the subsequent straight before it has actually finished rounding the bend (*33*). This is an important advantage, as it enables the driver to stop the rotational movement of the car and accelerate earlier, thereby getting a quicker run into the straight.

Obviously the sharper the turn, the more advantageous it is for the car to over-steer. Unfortunately, however, as we have demonstrated earlier, any tendency for the car to oversteer is decreased as the turn gets sharper and as the power applied to the rear driving

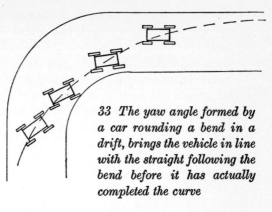

33 The yaw angle formed by a car rounding a bend in a drift, brings the vehicle in line with the straight following the bend before it has actually completed the curve

wheels increases. Thus, if a car is to be ideally suited to a sharp corner, rounding it with a slight tendency to oversteer, its tendency to oversteer on bends of greater radius which can be taken at high speed, will be considerably greater and make the vehicle difficult to drive. At the slightest turn of the steering wheel, the resulting centrifugal force will have the effect of rotating the car round its own axis more than is actually wanted. This will call for immediate correction by the driver. The car will respond to this but, due to its momentum, it will probably swing back past the position required, so that the driver will have to turn it back into the corner again and the car will thus proceed in a series of swerves.

High-speed stability being of primary importance, both for an ordinary touring vehicle and a competition car, most modern vehicles are designed to understeer to some degree. This is particularly important for a racing car that will be called upon to round fast curves at speeds in excess of 120 or 130 m.p.h., at the limit of adhesion, when it must be absolutely stable. Under such conditions any tendency to swerve would immediately cause the car to exceed the limit of adhesion and go off the road. This implies that it will understeer severely on sharper corners. The overall balance, however, remains beneficial for the understeering car, as on the average circuit more time is gained by going fast through fast bends than is lost on the slower ones. Moreover, provided he has sufficient power at his disposal, a competent driver of a rear-wheel-driven racing car can turn an understeering car into an oversteering one by applying sufficient torque to the driving wheels to make them reach the limit of adhesion under the combined action of the centrifugal force and driving torque. This action causes the rear wheels to slide out, their combined slide angle and slip angle adding up to a total greater than the slip angle of the front wheels. The car's basic understeer is thus turned into the controlled oversteer that is called a drift.

Drifting the Car Through the Bend

Only an understeering, rear-wheel-drive vehicle can be drifted. Drifting implies that, under the combined effects of the lateral component of the centrifugal force on the rear wheels and of the driving torque, the limit of adhesion is reached at the rear wheels before it is reached at the front wheels, which are subjected to the action of the lateral component of the centrifugal force only. In order to have the best control over the drift, it is necessary for the driver to have the greatest available torque that can be produced at the rear wheels immediately at his command. To achieve this he must select the proper gear before reaching the bend in which the car is to be drifted, so that the torque applied can be controlled precisely and immediately by the accelerator pedal. This is vitally important, as the drifting car is controlled as much by the driver's action upon the accelerator as by the steering wheel.

There is no clearly defined borderline between the so-called four-wheel drift and a proper slide or skid. In racing parlance, however, a car is usually said to be drifting when its front wheels are still more or less pointed in the direction of the bend to be taken, or, in marginal cases, are straight (*41*); the slide proper starts when the driver has to correct the line of progress by turning the front wheels into the opposite direction to the curve to be taken. From this it follows that only an understeering car can be drifted, as in most other cases the rear slip and slide angles will add up to such a total compared with the front slip angle, that the front wheels will have to be turned out slightly to compensate for the difference. If they must be turned out so much that they point in the opposite direction to the bend to be taken, the drift is turned into a slide or a skid.

The drift is the position which a properly designed understeering car assumes automatically when it is being cornered near the limit while sufficient torque is applied to the rear driving wheels—at least to keep up its speed. It is obviously dependent to a certain extent upon the ability and the judgement of the driver, but, within certain limits, it is a state of stable equilibrium. When

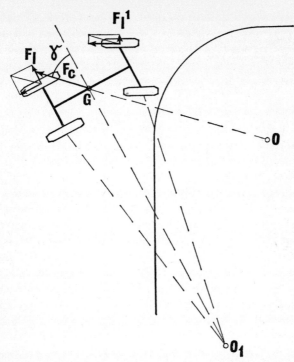

*34 Car in a four-wheel drift. The greater the yaw angle γ, the smaller be-
come the lateral components $F_l{}^1$ and F_l of the centrifugal F_c acting upon the
front and rear wheels, while the components acting backwards in the plane
of the wheels are increased*

a car rounds a curve at a speed low enough for the slip to be
negligible, the centre O of the curve it describes is in line with the
rear axle, where it is joined by the lines drawn at right angles to
the plane of the front wheels. As soon as slip and slide intervene,
however, this point does not correspond any more with the centre
of the actual curve taken by the vehicle. It moves to O_1 which
lies ahead of the centre of the rear axle. Figure 34 shows that if the
car were moving around the centre point O, that is without drifting or sliding, it would very soon hit the inside of the curve; in
actual fact it moves around O_1. This changes the direction of the
centrifugal force from OG to O_1G, where it forms a much smaller
angle in respect to the planes of the wheels. Assuming in both
cases the value of the centrifugal force to be identical, the value
of the component acting at a right angle to the wheel planes is

reduced. It gives rise, however, to a comparatively important component acting in the plane of the wheels and opposing the rolling motion of the car, tending to slow it.

As long as the driver does not modify the steering lock or the torque applied to the driving wheels, the car remains in a state of balance created by the various forces acting upon it. If, for any reason, the rear wheels were to drift out more, which would happen for instance if the driving torque were increased, thus decreasing the resistance of the rear axle to lateral forces, the car would assume a greater yaw angle (γ), thereby automatically reducing the component of the centrifugal force acting at right angles to the plane of the wheels, and increasing the component directed along their plane towards the rear, thereby automatically slowing the vehicle. A new state of equilibrium is thus achieved, the greater torque applied matching the increased rolling resistance of the car and the reduced lateral component of the centrifugal force being matched by the reduced lateral adhesion of the driving wheels due to the increased driving force transmitted. If the component of the centrifugal force acting in the plane of the rear wheels and the driving force necessary to keep the car going add up to a total at least equal to the adhesion of the rear wheels, there is no adhesion left to hold the wheels laterally and the car just spins out. The optimum value of the drift angle which must obviously exist between the extreme conditions where there is no drift and the ones reached when the car spins, is obtained when, for a bend of a given radius, the limit of adhesion of the driving, wheels is reached under the combined action of the lateral component of the centrifugal force and the driving force, for a driving force that is just sufficient to keep the car moving at the highest speed possible under the prevailing conditions. Up to now, for the sake of simplicity, we have assumed that the forward thrust put through the driving wheels inevitably reduced the resistance these wheels were able to oppose to forces acting at right angles to their plane, in the first instance the main component of the centrifugal force acting upon the car. This is quite correct, but it does not allow for the fact that any thrust put through the driving wheels causes a weight transfer from the front to the rear wheels.

Due to this weight transfer, the adhesion of the tyre on the road, which is proportional to the weight it carries, is increased, so that in the formula $F_l = \sqrt{(\text{Total Adhesion})^2 - F_p^2}$ (see page 52) F_l is not necessarily smaller than the adhesion of the tyre under static conditions. The increase in the weight carried—and thus of the total adhesion force available—under the influence of a driving force has a twofold origin. One is the reaction of the torque transmitted to the driving wheels, which is proportional to the torque and inversely proportional to the wheelbase of the car. The other is the inertia of the vehicle. The weight transfer to which it gives rise is proportional to the square of the vehicle's acceleration, proportional to the height of the centre of gravity and, again, inversely proportional to the wheelbase.

It can be shown that, up to a certain point, and due to the weight transfer, the ability for the rear driving wheels to resist sideway forces is actually increased when a driving force is put through them. If a greater force is transmitted, however, the ability to resist sideway forces is reduced again.

A driver who drifts his car through a bend instinctively finds this optimum condition where the maximum adhesion is available at the rear wheels to combat sideway forces. If, with the car in this condition, the throttle is shut suddenly, the weight transfer is reversed, increasing the load on the front wheels. As at the same moment the lateral component of the driving force acting upon them is also cancelled, they suddenly regain grip; their combined slide and slip angle is reduced to a much lower value than the drift angle at the rear wheels, creating a condition of violent oversteer, which will most likely send the car spinning off the track. As we will see, advantage can be taken of this to help an understeering car into a sharp corner.

The drift being, within certain limits, a state of equilibrium, it is comparatively easy for a competent driver to keep the car drifting along the desired line. The slight rear-wheel slide that, added to the slip, will put an understeering car at the required yaw angle can only be reached under the combined action of the centrifugal and driving forces. As long as the car is not turned into the bend, however, there is no centrifugal force acting upon it; moreover at the moment when it is turned into the curve, the inertia of the vehicle around its vertical axis, and the driving force which creates a component acting laterally upon the front wheels as soon as they are turned, combine to increase the tendency of the vehicle to understeer. The component of the driving force acting laterally upon the front wheels can be suppressed by releasing the throttle at the precise moment when the car is turned into the curve; the forces resulting from the vehicle's inertia around its vertical axis, however, can only be reduced, but never suppressed, by turning the car progressively into the curve.

This can easily be done when the car is driven into a fast curve, but is difficult when it enters a sharper corner. Here a racing car may show an embarrassing tendency to understeer that can only be counteracted effectively by turning the car into the corner while the brakes are still being applied moderately. The braking produces a weight transfer from the rear to the front axle, decreasing the former's adhesion in favour of the latter's, and thus encouraging the rear axle to slide out under the influence of the centrifugal force as soon as this reaches a high enough value. At this precise moment, the brakes must be released and the power applied, so as to keep the car drifting round the bend at the highest possible speed. This technique of initiating the drift by keeping the brakes slightly on while the car is turned into the bend, calls for extremely precise braking. If the car enters the corner a little too fast, and the brakes have to be applied a little too hard, a spin is almost inevitable; if conversely the speed is a little too low, or if to avoid slowing up the car too much the brakes are not kept applied until the vehicle is turned into the curve, it may be difficult to get the drift started.

The analysis of the forces acting upon a car rounding a bend makes it quite evident that a front-wheel-drive car cannot be drifted. Due to the driving torque applied to the front wheels and to the weight transfer which occurs under acceleration, decreasing the adhesion of the front wheels, it is inevitable that, if they are called upon to transmit a driving force, they will reach the limit of adhesion first and slide out under the effect of the centrifugal force. This means that the car will understeer and if, by applying more lock or reducing the torque transmitted by the front wheels, the car can, up to a certain point, be kept on the desired line, it can never be pointed in the direction of the exit of the curve before completing it, as does a drifting rear-wheel-drive car. This is an inherent disadvantage of a front-wheel-drive car as it means that full power for acceleration cannot be applied until the car has completely rounded the bend—that is at a later moment than is the case with a rear-wheel-drive car.

This disadvantage of front-wheel drive applies even in the case of small vehicles where the adhesion of the front wheels is adequate to transmit the available power. Front-wheel drive which, due to the reduced front-wheel adhesion under acceleration, is practical only for cars of moderate power-to-weight ratio, is at an advantage only on sharp corners. On these, the front-wheel lock is such that the driving force generated at the rear wheels of a rear-wheel-drive car gives rise to a lateral component acting upon the front wheels, which reduces their resistance to sliding more than the driving force that must be applied to the front wheels of an equivalent front-wheel-drive car, to get the same acceleration.

In conclusion, we can say that, due to the yaw angle taken up by a rear-wheel-drive car drifting round a corner, the component of the centrifugal force acting at a right angle to the wheel planes is reduced compared to what it would be if the yaw angle were nil, that is if the car cornered in a neutral attitude. Thanks to this, it can be cornered at a higher speed than it would if it remained neutral. As the yaw angle increases, however, so does the component of the centrifugal force acting along the longitudinal axis of the car and opposing its forward motion, until any further increase of the yaw angle causes the vehicle to stop rolling altogether and to slide broadside on to a stop or a crash.

Between cornering within the limits of adhesion with the car in a more or less neutral attitude and the broadside, there is a position for which the highest possible cornering speed is reached. It is up to the driver to find this position and to keep the car at the optimum yaw angle by means of judicious use of the steering wheel and the accelerator. This explains why, in racing, even though a car appears to be cornering perfectly steadily along a predetermined line, the driver is usually seen to be moving the steering wheel to and fro in rapid movements. What he does is merely to correct incipient slides tending to alter the yaw angle upon which he has settled. They are means to an end, not a means in themselves, as some people seem to think, who believe that for fast cornering it is essential to impart rapid alternate movements to the steering wheel. On the contrary, the best driver is the one who is able to detect any unwanted movement of the car while it is still so small that it can be rectified by a mere touch of the steering wheel. A real top-rank driver can feel what the car is going to do even before it has started to do it, and act accordingly. Recourse to large movements of the steering wheel to keep the car on its course, is the hallmark of a bad driver.

CHAPTER V

FROM THEORY TO PRACTICE

Emergency Line

UNDER racing or rallying conditions, circumstances may often make it impossible strictly to apply the rules dictated by theory. Other road users must be considered, even on the racing track where faster cars may pass you, or slower cars must be passed which may momentarily bring you off your chosen line. Passing in itself may be quite a problem when the car to be overtaken and the one you are driving are evenly matched and, above all, there is the human factor. Motor racing is a very exacting sport and the slightest error of judgement, even if it does not always result in a catastrophe, may cause serious trouble.

When a driver gets really pressed, one way for him to save split seconds is to leave his braking before a corner as late as possible. Under such circumstances, it is inevitable that it will eventually be left too late. If the driver nevertheless persists in taking his normal line, the car will come into the corner too fast and will most probably go off the road or spin. The only way for the driver to extricate himself from this difficult situation is to aim the car at the inside of the curve as soon as he realises that he will not be able to slow the car sufficiently to take the bend in the normal way (35). In this way the car can be kept on a more or less straight line for a slightly longer distance and the brakes can be kept fully applied for a longer time before the car is turned into the corner. This line will result in a sharper curve round the corner which will thus have to be taken at a slightly slower speed, but at least the worst will have been avoided. On balance it is not even certain that this method, systematically applied, results in a waste of time, as what may be lost on the bend itself, may be made up by the slightly later braking which this unorthodox line makes possible. Very few drivers take advantage of this possibility, but among its adherents is no less a driver than Stirling Moss, who says

that if it does not save
time, at least it is a
safer line because it
leaves more road on the
outside of the bend to
fight the car if an error
of judgement has been
made. Of course, this
method is also very use-
ful in rallies where roads
are open to the ordinary
traffic and it is not
feasible or permissible

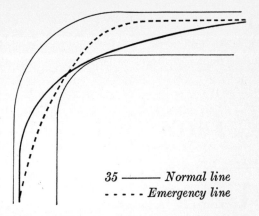

35 ———— *Normal line*
- - - - - *Emergency line*

to use its full width, especially on the approach to a blind corner.
It can be used on right-hand bends on the Continent and in
America, where the rule of the road is to drive on the right and
on left-hand bends in England and other countries where the rule
is to drive on the left.

Up to now we have always assumed the road to be the only
sort of surface upon which a racing car may be driven. Keen
observers of motor racing, however, will no doubt have noticed
that many racing drivers think otherwise and cut some corners
to the extent that the inner wheels of their cars cut across the verge
of the road whenever it is reasonably level with the latter. The
fact that the surface of the verge may be rougher than the road
surface is of little importance in view of the fact that the inside
wheels of a car that is being cornered at the limit bear very little
weight, and this method has the double advantage of cutting a
shorter way across the corner and enabling the driver to straighten
the line he takes through it, thus raising the speed at which it can
be taken. The fact that dust and stones are also raised and thrown
in the face of the man behind is an incidental, but admittedly
worth-while, advantage. . . !

Overtaking

One of the main problems which arise from having a number of
cars racing on the same circuit is that, on bends and corners, one
single car uses up the entire width of the road. This means that
when two cars are racing side by side along a straight, one must
give way to the other when they come up to the next corner. The
rule normally applicable in motor racing—that one should drive

on the right and pass on the left—does not strictly apply to corners, where it is common practice to pass where it is safer or easier to do so. The question arises therefore which of two cars racing neck and neck towards a corner has right of way over the other? The answer is: the one who gets there first or the one who is best placed to nip into the corner first. Of the two drivers, one may have slightly stronger nerves and leave his braking until a few yards later, which will give him the advantage and enable him to get in front; if braking does not bring about a decision, then the driver who holds the inside position has the obvious advantage of being able to take a shorter course and therefore the corner is his. At any time *before* a driver has set his car on a given line for a corner, other drivers may try and get an advantage over him; but once a car is set on its line, it is *not* permissible to cut across it and force the other driver to alter his course, which could have disastrous results.

But where then, it will be asked, can a better driver pass a slower competitor driving a car of equal performance, if this cannot be done on corners where the better driver can use his ability to the best advantage? One answer has already been given: in the braking area preceding a corner. If one driver goes round the corner slower than the other, he must of necessity brake earlier and this will give the better driver a chance to pass him in the braking area. However, this is feasible only before slow corners where the braking area is long enough for the passing to be performed. In other cases, the better driver who has been unable to pass before the corner will be baulked by the slower driver and will have to take the corner at the same slower speed. Assuming both cars to have equal performance, the driver behind will not be able to pass his rival before the next corner, where the same story will repeat itself and cost the better driver a lot of valuable time. Unless the circuit includes a straight long enough to offer an opportunity of passing by taking advantage of the slipstream of the car in front, the only chance of passing a slower driver whose car matches the performance of your own, is to slow down and let him take a lead corresponding to what you think you can gain on him in the next corner. This will prevent you from being baulked and, having taken the bend faster, you will leave it faster and easily pass the other car before it has picked up enough speed to match yours.

The third method of passing is—as has been hinted at before—

slipstreaming. An area of reduced air pressure is produced behind any car that is being driven at high speed; this reduced pressure will lessen the air drag of a car that is being driven close behind, thus increasing its speed. Slower cars can take advantage of this to 'get a tow' from faster cars, and in the case of two cars of identical maximum speed following each other, the second one will quickly close up on the first, thanks to the reduced air resistance. If its driver pulls out at the last possible moment, he will be able to pass the first car before air drag reduces his speed to its normal maximum.

The Importance of Proper Gearing

As we have already seen, in order to get the car round a bend or a corner as quickly as possible, it is essential that when it enters the corner, the driver can call upon the highest possible torque at the driving wheels. In this way he will be in the best possible position to keep the car drifting round the bend and will be able to use the greatest acceleration available as soon as conditions permit. In order to achieve this he must, before entering the corner, select the gear that will produce the highest possible driving torque. This sounds easier than it sometimes actually is, especially when it comes to going fast on an unknown road, as is often the case in rallies. Frequently the exact shape of the road that lies ahead cannot be properly assessed, and in such circumstances many drivers tend to select the next lower gear, just in case it will be needed. In my opinion this is wrong, as experience has shown in at least five out of six cases where the issue is in doubt, the lower gear is not actually required. Using it brings the speed down unnecessarily; changing down and up again wastes precious time and the use of the lower gear stresses the engine unnecessarily. In such circumstances, it is undoubtedly better to keep the higher gear engaged, see what happens around the corner, and change if really necessary, as soon as conditions permit—at the latest at the exit of the bend. Of course time will have been lost, but on balance, considering the number of unnecessary gear changes which will be saved, this method results in an overall saving of time.

The same principle applies also to circuit racing, even though in this case the driver knows exactly where he is going, and at what speed any bend on the circuit can be taken. He may be in doubt, however, as to which gear to use for a given corner where the car appears to be a bit sluggish on a comparatively high gear, but where the engine will be kept quite near its revolution limit on the next lower gear, calling for an early change up. Here again the answer is: 'In case of doubt, use the higher gear; it will save time and the engine.' Time will be saved not only because any gear change costs time—about a car's length—but also because every time a driver has to change down for a corner, his concentration is distracted from the road for a moment and he instinctively increases the safety margin and goes slower.

Less Braking—More Speed

If you want to go fast, keep off the brakes! I will never forget a scene I witnessed at Spa during practice for the Belgian Grand Prix of 1953. The Maserati factory had entered four cars—three for the regular team of Fangio, Gonzalez and Bonetto, and a fourth car for the former Belgian champion, the late Johnny Claes. Try as he might, Claes could not nearly match the times of Fangio and Gonzalez. After much fruitless hard trying, Claes, who was a close friend of Fangio's, approached him and asked him if he would try his car because he thought it was slower than the others. Fangio immediately agreed; he jumped into Claes's car and did three or four laps, the fastest of which was just about as fast as he had done in his own car. When Fangio came back into the pits, Claes shrugged his shoulders and said, 'But tell me, how on earth do you do it?' Fangio said nothing at first and extricated himself from the cockpit; he then went quietly to sit on the pit counter, with Claes following him and, in his broken English, gave his very plain and simple explanation: 'Less brakes,' he said, 'and more accelerator.'

The assertion that speed is increased as less use is made of the brakes is, of course, a fallacy. To go fast, the brakes must be used, and used very hard indeed, but only where it is essential to slow the car down. For obvious reasons, much more unnecessary use is made of the brakes on the road than on a circuit which the driver knows perfectly. On the road any driver has a strong instinctive tendency to use his brakes as soon as he is not absolutely sure of what lies ahead. More concentration and better observation of any signs which may give a clue as to what is coming up, will help reduce the number of unnecessary applications of the brakes and enable the speed to be maintained at a higher average. To achieve high road averages, it is essential first of all to concentrate on avoiding unnecessary braking and it certainly takes a lot of concentration before this becomes a natural habit. But while it saves time, it also helps to save tyres, brakes and fuel. It can confidently be said that the merit of a driver is inversely proportional to the number of times he applies his brakes unnecessarily for a given mileage.

CHAPTER VI

PRACTICE

Practising for a Circuit Race

AS a driver I have always felt that the practice periods before a race meeting are much more interesting and enjoyable than the race itself. Maybe this is partly because I am a strong individualist and like to go out and start as and when I feel like it. Another important reason is that I am extremely interested in the technical aspect of racing and pay much attention to the preparation of the car and its adaptation to the particular conditions prevailing on the circuit under consideration. This is a very important aspect of the pre-race practice.

Before the car is taken care of, however, the driver must become truly familiar with the circuit. If the driver is new to the circuit, it is a good policy wherever possible to go round the circuit with a normal touring car for several laps before the first practice session begins, so as to know at least where the corners are, watching out for any likely source of danger, and also taking note of any possible escape roads. Some circuits like the Nürburgring, which is fourteen miles long and boasts 174 bends and corners, take a lot of learning. It is difficult for a driver new to it to learn the 'Ring' during the official pre-race practice; even if it were possible, the mileage involved would completely wear out a racing car. This is the exception rather than the rule, however, and on the usual shorter circuits the time available is normally sufficient for a driver to learn the course perfectly, without straining his car excessively. As he gets to know the course better, improving his line through the various corners, the driver laps faster and faster. He increases his average speed by taking the bends and corners at a higher speed, which he does by braking progressively later or even deciding that he can take some of the bends without braking at all, or without even lifting his foot from the accelerator. To start with, the driver uses his own judgement to decide where he must brake for a corner,

70

but as soon as he seeks to reduce his braking distance, he starts looking for anything that can serve him as a marker on the road-side, showing the exact point where to apply the brakes. On most circuits the organisers put up signs at 100, 200, and 300 metre or yard intervals at the approach to the various bends, which considerably help the drivers as they seek progressively to reduce their braking distance, and enable them, when they have reached their target, to repeat the performance on every successive lap.

Some corners may involve a problem for a driver new to them. Not all are ideally shaped or regularly banked. Some may have an irregular contour, a decreasing or an increasing radius, or, in fact, be made up of a succession of two or more bends in the same direction, which are best taken in one single sweep. In such cases, the correct line through the corner does not necessarily bring the car nearest to the inside verge more or less half-way through the bend, and the correct point to aim at is not always easy to find. Figures 36, 37 and 38 show three examples of such curves.

If the driver finds he loses time on a particular portion of the circuit because he has failed to find the best line through it, he should not hesitate, after the end of the first practice session, to inspect it thoroughly on foot, in order to understand the exact shape of the road and to try to visualize the line along which it should be negotiated. Once he has decided on the line that should give the best results, he should try to find some landmark, as close as possible to the inside verge, at which to aim his car, to make sure that he keeps to his predetermined line. When practice is resumed, however, he should try his new line at a comparatively modest speed, to make sure that everything goes according to plan, and then go progressively faster. Never decide to change your line without trying the new one at a slightly reduced speed first!

In the course of practice, the driver will also have found out which gear is best for any particular section of the circuit. Once he has learned the circuit well enough to get a good run into its various straights, he can also judge if the overall gearing of the vehicle is suitable. The lower the gearing, the faster the car will accelerate. The choice of final gear ratio should be governed by the r.p.m. reached by the engine on the fastest part of the circuit, when the oil in the engine and transmission have worked up to their normal temperature. Basically the ratio is correct if, in top gear, the engine can reach the highest permissible figure. If this is not attained, it means that as the gearing is too high, the engine

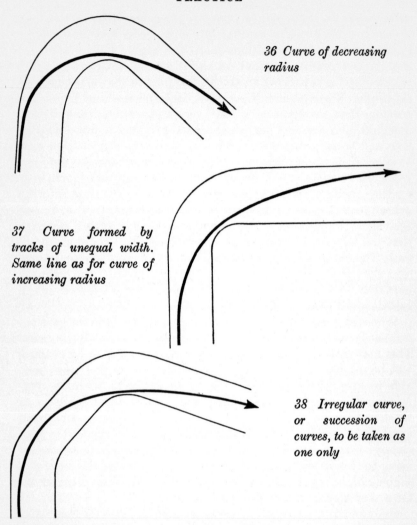

36 Curve of decreasing radius

37 Curve formed by tracks of unequal width. Same line as for curve of increasing radius

38 Irregular curve, or succession of curves, to be taken as one only

is not able to produce its maximum power, and not only will acceleration suffer everywhere on the circuit, but the car will not reach the highest maximum speed of which it is capable on that particular circuit. On the other hand, if the engine tends to exceed its maximum permissible revolution rate, the driver will have to lift off the accelerator slightly in order not to damage the engine and again maximum speed will suffer. This rule must not be adhered to dogmatically, however, and there are cases where it pays deliberately to undergear or overgear. In a very long race, where maximum speed will be held for quite a considerable time—as for instance the Le Mans 24 hours race—the engine will be saved by slightly overgearing, so that on the three-mile-long straight the engine speed is kept down to about 300 r.p.m. below the permissible maximum. The Spa circuit on the other hand is a case for undergearing. Here a several-miles-long, very fast stretch slopes slightly downhill, and another part of the circuit, which is just about as long and equally fast, slopes very slightly uphill; in neither case however is the slope steep enough to justify the use of two different gears, for instance fifth gear for the downhill part and fourth gear for the uphill stretch. It is thus necessary to compromise with the overall gear ratio and experience has shown that it is best to choose the most suitable ratio for the slightly uphill part, even if it means that the driver will have to lift his foot slightly on the downhill part. The performance on the uphill stretch is much more important than the very slight gain in maximum speed on the downhill part that could be obtained by gearing higher and which could be sustained for only a very few seconds.

When, after a practice session, it is decided to alter the gearing, it must be remembered that the alteration applies to all the gears. This may well mean that more, or sometimes less, gear changes will be needed on every lap. If, for example, you had just been able to keep in second gear between two corners, without over-revving the engine, lowering the gearing will inevitably force you to change up to third for a few yards before you change back again into second for the next corner, and these two extra gear changes may well cost you as much time as you save elsewhere by using the lower gearing. Conversely, you may well decide to use a slightly higher gear just to dispense with the need of changing up for a very short while in a particular case.

On circuits in which a long straight is included, you may want systematically to take advantage of the slipstream of some faster cars, in order to increase the maximum speed of yours. If your car is correctly geared for normal conditions, the speed increase gained by other cars' slipstreams will send the engine revving several hundred r.p.m. above its permissible maximum. To avoid this, a slightly higher gear must be chosen than would normally be used if slipstreaming were not taken into consideration.

In cases where only a very small adjustment of the gearing is called for, it can usually be achieved by using a different tyre or

73

rim size. It must be remembered, however, that the use of a different tyre size may affect the behaviour of the car, and that small tyres reach a higher temperature and wear out quicker than bigger ones.

Tyres are another point which must be watched attentively during practice. If the race is to be a long one, or if the circuit is hard on tyres, their wear must be studied closely. Even for shorter races this may be quite useful, as racing cars usually handle best on part-worn tyres; so if the rate of wear permits, it may be better not to start on new tyres. If new tyres are called for, however, they should at least be rubbed in during practice, so as to remove the glossy and slippery skin. The rate of wear is calculated by measuring the depth of the tyre profile before and after practice and relating it to the number of laps completed at racing speed.

It is now common practice for racing tyre manufacturers to produce special tyres giving better grip on wet road surfaces. This is usually done by using a different rubber mixture giving better adhesion but which wears quicker if it is used on a dry road surface. This mixture also generates more heat, due to its higher hysteresis, and if rain tyres are used for fast races in the dry, the treads may come off under the effect of the centrifugal force—with obviously dangerous results. Rain tyres may also slightly affect the handling of the car on dry roads, for the better or for the worse. In any case they should be tried for a few laps in practice, even if the weather is dry, if only to rub them in in case they are needed for the race.

Another very important point to be checked in practice is the fuel consumption. The fuel mileage may vary quite considerably according to the circuit on which the car is running and to the gear ratio it calls for. As in competitive motoring, the engine is kept in its maximum power range as much as possible, its consumption is more closely related to the time elapsed than to the mileage covered by the car.

Starting positions are usually decided by practice times. The only important race with a massed start in which this does not apply is the Le Mans 24 hours race, in order that competitors are not tempted to overstress their cars which will have to face another 24 hours' hard racing. Moreover, in a race of such duration, starting positions have no possible bearing whatsoever on the final results.

In short races, however, starting positions are very important, as cars and drivers are not only very closely matched, but everyone must more or less go as fast as he can right from the start, as this sort of race is usually won by seconds—sometimes even split seconds—rather than minutes. Passing in these conditions becomes very difficult, seconds lost in the process are very hard to make up, and the man who is able to take the lead or, at least, to lead his nearest rivals right from the start, is at a considerable advantage.

In some races, much more is at stake than a mere starting position—when the qualification of the driver is dependent upon the best time he can put up in practice. In such a case, it is very important that, if the first day of practice is dry, the driver should do a sufficient number of laps to become really familiar with the circuit. He should then stop and relax, have his car thoroughly checked and set out towards the end of the practice period, when the track is comparatively empty, to do five or six laps as fast as he can. He should do this even if, for example, he thinks the gearing is not absolutely right, as the next day may be wet, making it difficult for him to achieve a time good enough to get a good starting position or to qualify. Potentially faster cars or drivers who, for some reason, have been unable to go fast or who were absent on the first day, may also find it impossible to better his qualifying time if the second day is wet.

Obviously, in order to achieve the best possible performance, the car should be as lightly laden as possible, with the tanks just sufficiently full to last the number of laps the driver sets out to do, with a fairly safe margin.

And, if your car is not one of the fastest on the track, split seconds, or on really fast circuits such as Spa, Le Mans or Rheims, even several full and very valuable seconds, can be saved by cunningly waiting for a faster car to overtake, and then taking advantage of its slipstream.

At Indianapolis, where the qualification runs, over four timed laps of the track, take place for each car separately and up to nearly three weeks before the race, entrants go to such lengths as using special gear ratios, special fuels, higher compression and sometimes even fuel injection on engines normally fed by carburettors, to make sure of qualifying. In that state of tune, the cars would not stand the slightest chance of lasting even through the first quarter of the 500 miles race, but they usually survive the qualification runs. If they do not, there is always enough time left for repairs and to have another go.

The practice period is also the time to check that the car is handling properly and is correctly suited to the circuit on which it is to run. Several means of adjusting the handling characteristics are usually provided on modern racing cars, and even production touring cars are responsive to some simple forms of treatment.

Factors Affecting the Handling of the Car

The basic handling characteristics of a motor vehicle are mainly influenced by the following factors:

(1) Its main dimensions.
(2) Its weight distribution and the height of its centre of gravity.
(3) The geometry of its front and rear suspensions.
(4) The roll resistance of its front and rear suspensions.
(5) The front and rear tyre characteristics and pressures.

Some of these factors can be altered to suit the preference of individual drivers. The easiest way to alter the handling of a car is to adjust the tyre pressures. If a car oversteers too much, it may be possible to reduce this tendency by increasing the pressure of the rear tyres or decreasing the pressure in the front tyres, or both. By doing this, the slip angle under given conditions is decreased at the rear and increased at the front. Conversely, if a car understeers too much, the remedy is to increase the front tyre pressure and decrease the rear tyre pressure. This has quite an appreciable effect with touring cars, where pressures of between 15 and 25 lbs per square inch are used, but the effect is reduced at racing pressures ranging from 30 to 45 lbs per square inch. Moreover, there is a limit beyond which the pressure cannot be decreased any further as this would lead to prohibitive overheating of the tyre, and to an intolerable increase of the rolling resistance. Excessive pressure on the other hand, will lead to wheel bounce and reduced adhesion on bumpy surfaces. Where the rules permit, the slip angle under given conditions can be reduced by using a fatter tyre mounted on a wider rim. If this combination is mounted at the rear, the tendency to oversteer will be reduced, or the tendency to understeer increased.

The effect upon the attitude of the car of modifying the setting of the shock absorbers is limited to the transitory stage where the car is being turned into the curve or out of it. Harder shock absorbers will momentarily offer a greater resistance to roll until the roll angle dictated by the forces acting upon the suspension

39 Phil Hill's and the late W. von Trips' severely understeering Ferraris follow Brabham's approximately neutral steering Cooper-Climax in the 1960 French Grand Prix at Rheims

40 Very strong oversteer, amplified by excessive wheel spin, is displayed here by Jack Brabham's Cooper-Climax. Time is lost rather than gained by 'fireworks' of this sort

41 *Jack Brabham again, but this time performing a perfect piece of cornering. His Cooper-Climax is held in a copybook four-wheel drift, with the front wheels dead straight, the car being kept in the turn by the fact that perfect throttle control keeps the rear wheels drifting out just a little bit more than the front ones. This is the fastest way of getting around a bend*

42 *Big sports and G.T. cars, which have a higher centre of gravity and are much heavier in relation to the size of their tyres, assume a much greater drift angle than modern G.P. cars, as is shown here by W. Mairesse's and O. Gendebien's Ferrari 250 G.T.s at Spa, in 1960*

system has been reached, after which they have no further effect upon roll stiffness. Sometimes, however, this momentary effect can be quite useful—to make a car that understeers too much more sensitive, for example, which can be done by increasing the stiffness of the rear shock absorbers. Of course, shock-absorber settings have a notable effect upon the behaviour of the car on indifferent road surfaces by checking wheel bounce and providing more constant adhesion. But if their setting is too hard, the dampers will interfere with the proper work of the suspension and adversely affect the handling.

Altering the tyre pressure and the shock-absorber settings are about the only modifications the normal private owner of an ordinary touring car is likely to undertake in order to modify the cornering characteristics of his vehicle. If serious competition work is contemplated, however, and if it is felt that the cornering characteristics of the car are not satisfactory, it may be worth while to undertake further modifications. A stronger anti-roll bar may be used at the front if more understeer is required or at the rear if it is felt that the car understeers too much; if only one anti-roll bar is fitted as standard, another may be added as necessary. Similar effects may be obtained by using stiffer springs at the front or at the rear, but it must be remembered that this will also affect the suspension. To avoid pitching, it is necessary for the front-spring rate to be lower than the rear-spring rate, so it is not advisable to use stiffer springs at the front without also increasing the stiffness of the rear springs. But a slight increase in the stiffness of the rear springs to reduce understeer may be a good and simple alternative to fitting a rear anti-roll bar. On cars using a rear suspension by swinging half axles, a slight difference in the height of the springs can have a considerable influence upon the vehicle's behaviour. This is due to the fact that any up-and-down motion of the body modifies the camber of the rear wheels. Thus by reducing the spring height, the camber angle is reduced and may even become negative, thereby lessening the slip angle of the rear wheels under any given conditions of lateral force, weight and tyre pressure. Shortening the rear springs will therefore combat the tendency to oversteer which characterises cars using a rear suspension by swinging half axles. It should be borne in mind, however, that this will also have the effect of reducing the spring travel and the suspension will probably have a bad tendency to bottom on rough roads, under laden conditions. With this type of suspension, only shock absorbers with a strong differential setting, damping the rebound action much more than the bump, should be used, as they tend to pull the springs down under normal driving conditions.

On modern racing cars, there is much more scope for altering the handling characteristics than on normal touring or production sports cars. On racing cars, several alternative pivot points for the suspension linkage are usually provided so that the height of the roll centre and the suspension geometry can be altered to choice (47). In most cases there are also means of adjusting the wheel camber front and rear and the toe-in of the rear wheels can be adjusted as well as that of the front wheels. Giving the rear wheels some toe-in will provide a steering effect by the wheel carrying the greater weight—that is, the outside wheel on a bend. It is used in some cases to promote understeer, but it should be remembered that any toe-in or -out of the front or rear wheels has the undesirable effect of increasing the rolling resistance. It also obviously increases the tyre wear while much harm can also be done to the tyres by excessive negative camber. This concentrates the car's weight on a small band of only half, or even only one-third, of the full tread's width, which thus wears quicker and can reach very high temperatures indeed. On the 1961 Grand Prix Ferraris, which used a negative camber of at least 5 degrees, temperature differences of up to 70° centigrade were measured between the inner and the outer part of the tread on very fast circuits such as Spa and Rheims, and some trouble was experienced with parts of the tread being flung off by centrifugal force. For this reason one should try to obtain the desired handling characteristics, without recourse to any drastic toe-in or adverse camber. Once a satisfactory set-up has been obtained, it should not be necessary to make any further major adjustment to adapt the car to various circuits. Usually the car can be made to understeer less for the slower circuits or more for the faster circuits by merely adjusting the tyre pressures, fitting or removing anti-roll bars, or making very slight adjustments to the wheel camber. Decreasing the camber of the front wheels by no more than $\frac{3}{4}$ of a degree, to check severe understeer on two slow corners, had the quite remarkable effect of decreasing the lap times of my Cooper by two full seconds, that is by almost exactly 2%, during practice for the 1960 South African Grand Prix in East London.

CHAPTER VII

SPEED AND SAFETY

AT speeds of around 150 miles per hour, which is well below the maximum speed of many racing cars, a car travels about 200 feet in every second, needs about 800 feet to stop, and will travel 40 feet in 1/5th of a second, i.e. in the normal reaction time of a trained driver. This means that if anything unforeseen were to happen, the car could easily have left the road before the driver was able to take any action whatsoever. High speeds can thus only be indulged in safely if the driver uses adequate foresight.

Circuit drivers who have an intimate knowledge of the course they drive on, and know that it is most unlikely for them to find any obstacle in their way other than rival racing cars, running at approximately the same speed as theirs, do not look nearly as far ahead as they would if they were driving at the same speed on the open road. All the time their minds are devoted to placing the car correctly for the hazard they are about to negotiate, but all the same they must keep an eye on the other cars and watch out for any situation that might lead to an incident, or perhaps an accident, in which they might become involved. *The ability to antici-pate, not the reaction time, is what matters most in the making of a safe, fast driver.* Not only must he know how his own car is going to react in any given circumstance—perhaps it is going to start a skid—and take corrective action even before it has begun to do so, but he must be able to observe, for instance, that the man in front has gone into a corner a little too fast, or has come off his normal line, and be prepared for the result, trying to figure out for himself in a fraction of a second, what the other car is going to do— maybe in which direction it is going to shoot off and how he could best avoid it. Only a highly developed sense of anticipation has kept Fangio out of trouble where other drivers were involved in multiple crashes. One of these happened at Monza in the 1953 Italian Grand Prix when Ascari and Farina were leading him to the finishing line on the last lap when they were brought off their line by another driver and both crashed. Fangio, who was racing just behind, immediately weighed up the situation and was able to avoid both the crashing cars and win the race. Another example is the disastrous Le Mans race of 1955 when Levegh's Mercedes crashed from behind into Macklin's Austin-Healey and killed 85 spectators; Fangio was coming up just behind and was able to drive through the mêlée to safety. A third instance is the multiple crash in the Monte Carlo Grand Prix of 1957 when, on the second lap, with all cars still bunched together, Moss, who was in the lead crashed into a barrier and Hawthorn and Collins, who were following close behind, were unable to avoid being involved in the accident. Even though the road was getting more and more blocked as the cars piled up one after the other, Fangio, who was close behind, again managed to steer his Maserati clear and to victory.

Important as anticipation may be on a track, it is much more so, indeed it is vital, on the less known or unknown roads, which are usually also unguarded, with which rally drivers are usually faced. It is here that the so-called road sense comes in. This may best be described as the faculty for a driver to have his attention attracted immediately by anything that might lead to a change of situation, calling for action to be taken in order to save time, or in the interest of his own or other road users' safety. An experienced driver is very seldom forced to take emergency action; for him emergencies practically never arise.

There is no substitute for experience, but a receptive mind can collect a lot of experience in a comparatively short time and will soon learn where to look out for danger. You cannot look everywhere at the same time, so your eyes and your mind must dismiss at once, and forget, anything that is not of immediate interest, in order the better to concentrate on more important things. The ability to distinguish immediately between what is important and what is not, can be trained to the point where, out of two dozen people walking or standing on the pavement, you will be able immediately to pick out the one person who is going to cross in front of your car. Many people would be surprised if they knew how much can sometimes be deduced from how little. For instance, a long shadow may herald the approach of a car at crossroads before the actual car can be seen; the fraction of a second that elapses between the moment where the shadow appears and the car can actually be seen may spell the difference between a safe stop and a crash. If, on the other hand, you see pedestrians calmly walking across a crossroad, you may safely assume that no vehicle is about to appear. And if they suddenly jump for their lives, you certainly can draw your own conclusions! In town, shop windows may also reflect a vehicle before you can actually see it—and they can also be very useful when it comes to parking a car in a confined space between two other vehicles.

A car may be stopped on the roadside; your first glance must be for its interior. If it is occupied, people may open a door and step out on to the road; if the driver is at the wheel, the car may start or even turn round. If it is a lorry, it may hide a man whose legs you can probably see if you look under the vehicle.

What is important is to know where to look, when to look and what to look for. In town, when another car preceding yours makes a crash stop, compelling you to use your brakes very hard yourself, your reflex should be not to stand on the brake pedal and push it as hard as you can, but rather to use your brakes as smoothly as conditions permit and stop as near the car in front as possible, in order to give the man behind a chance to stop himself without crashing into your car. As soon as you know you have matters under control, give a glance in the driving mirror to see what is happening behind; maybe it will warrant pulling out to the right or left, if there is room to do so, so that the driver following you gets a chance to cope with the situation.

On increasingly crowded roads, an ever larger number of accidents take the form of multiple collisions of cars being driven in a queue and bumping one into the other when for some reason one of them is brought to a quick stop. Even if you keep a reasonable distance between your car and the one in front, it is absolutely impossible for you to stop in time to avoid hitting it if its normal braking distance is shortened by crashing into another car! This is no excuse, however; a driver must be prepared for that sort of foreseeable incident to happen. Instead of watching only the car ahead of him, he must try to see the vehicle running two or three positions in front so that action can be taken early enough to avoid that sort of crash. In this position he will also have the advantage of occupying a position slightly offset in relation to the car in front, which will facilitate an emergency manœuvre if it is called for.

You may ask what these examples of anticipation which increase driving safety, and are a basic requirement for any good driver, have to do with competition driving. True, not all of them apply to track racing, but rally drivers are faced with all the hazards of normal traffic, and the slightest incident will inevitably mean the loss of much valuable time, not to mention the fact that a competitor in a sporting event will draw suspicion upon himself, even if this is entirely unjustified. In most of these cases, safety also goes hand in hand with speed.

There are few occasions where foresight and good judgement can save as much time as when passing other cars on the road. Coming up behind a slower vehicle, where the road is not wide enough for three cars to be driven abreast safely, you first have to make the decision whether you can pass safely, or if oncoming traffic will force you to slow until the road is cleared. Once this important decision is taken, and if you have decided to stay behind, it is very important accurately to judge the speed of the other two vehicles, and adjust the progress of your car in such a way that you come up behind the vehicle to be overtaken at the highest possible speed, just at the moment when the oncoming vehicle has cleared the road (43). The earlier you slow down, the less

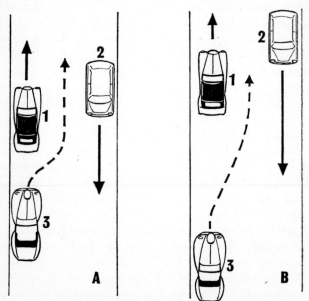

43 Overtaking with oncoming traffic
A *Incorrect*   B *correct*

84

your speed will have to be reduced and the quicker your former cruising speed can be regained. Having no control over the speed of the other two vehicles, the spot where they will pass each other is a predetermined point and the faster your speed when you pull out to overtake, the better the run-in you get into the next stretch of road. If you do not reduce speed soon enough, you will have to brake down to a slower speed, maybe even down to the speed of the vehicle to be overtaken, and then pick up from that speed as the road is cleared. If, thanks to good judgement, your former cruising speed of 100 miles per hour is reduced only to 80 before you can pick up again, it will take a good sports car only about 15 to 20 seconds to regain its former cruising gait; if bad judgement compels you to slow down to 30 miles per hour before you can pick up again, it will take about twice the time to regain the original cruising speed. Such quite unnecessary losses of 15 to 20 seconds quickly add up to several minutes and may well spell the difference between keeping to a tight schedule and losing marks.

Foresight may also help save the car and the suspension system from severe road shocks such as may be caused by pot-holes, a gully running across the road or a hump-back. Such hazards may be difficult to recognise sufficiently early to check the speed to a rate where the car will run over them smoothly; or you may have to maintain too tight a schedule to permit slowing down as much as you would like. Nevertheless, you must remember that braking increases the load on the front suspension, which must bear not only an increased weight, but also the brake torque reaction. On most cars, braking also creates a nose-dipping movement that reduces the upward travel of the front suspension and its ability to absorb road shocks. The suspension should therefore be relieved of all additional strain induced by the action of the brakes, by releasing the brakes just before it is called upon to absorb a severe shock. It is even possible to time the release of the brakes in such a way that the rebound of the suspension resulting from it increases the upward range of travel of the wheels at the precise moment when it is most wanted for the absorption of the impact. In this way a car can be made to jump an obstacle to a certain extent.

Foresight and observation will also enable you to drive fast and safely on the open road where visibility is scanty. Where the road disappears beyond the crest of a hill or a major hump, trees or telegraph poles, or in some countries advertisement hoardings, may give you a clue to the direction it takes where it cannot be seen and enable you to place the car correctly to negotiate the stretch fast and safely. Nearing the crest of a rise, you may come up behind another car which it does not seem safe to overtake because the crest may be hiding a vehicle coming in the opposite direction. The answer may well be given by road users travelling in the same direction as yours. If, for example, some way beyond the crest, the roof of a car preceding you can be seen, you may assume that if a vehicle were coming in the opposite direction you should also see its roof and that it is therefore safe for you to overtake. Or if on the crest of a hill, or leaving a blind corner, a driver in front pulls out to overtake, you may assume that the road is free and do so yourself. Even if the other driver has acted wrongly, his car will serve you as a protecting screen against any possible oncoming traffic. And, of course, difficult roads winding up or down the side of a mountain can often be observed over quite long distances, so that the opportunity should never be lost to spot vehicles coming the other way and to be prepared to make room for them when the time comes.

Seat Belts

Whatever the precautions taken, whatever the skill of the driver, fast driving involves risks. Indeed if we motor at all, we accept a reasonable, but none the less undeniable risk. Nobody's judgement is infallible; on the road, the driver of an oncoming car may collapse at the precise moment the cars are about to pass each other and unavoidably cut across your path, or some fool may dart out of a small forest track into the main road slap across your bows.

If the impact is unavoidable, how do you stand the best chance of escaping major injury? In a standard production closed car, the body structure is usually strong enough to stand up to the impact, at least to the extent of not crushing its occupants inside, unless the car hits a solid obstacle at high speed or another car head-on. Any injuries sustained by the driver and his passengers will most likely be caused by hitting some hardware inside the body as they are thrown forward out of their seats, or as the car rolls over.

That sort of car certainly asks for seat belts, and many experiments have demonstrated that they considerably reduce the risk of injury. These tests have also shown that the lap belts of the sort used in air liners are not sufficient, as they do not prevent the body from dropping forward and the head from making contact with the steering wheel, the dash or, in the case of rear-seat passengers, the front-seat squab. A diagonal belt, firmly secured to the car's structure, at shoulder height on one side, and to the floor on the other side of the seat, gives much better results, though the possibility remains that the underbody of the occupant will slide forward under the impact and be thrown against the dash. The safest type of belt is really a combination of lap and diagonal belts which will retain the driver or passenger in the seat wherever the impact comes from. From the safety point of view, the only important disadvantage of seat belts is that, in the case of fire, a quick-action clip must be released before one can get out of the car.

Whatever the type of belt used, they undoubtedly limit the freedom of movement—if not in the course of ordinary driving, then when the driver or passenger has to reach forward or sideways for controls, switches, maps and so forth. Rally competitors may thus elect to use the belts only where the schedule is tight, but it is absolutely necessary for a passenger in a rally to secure himself whenever he wants to take some rest or sleep. As he cannot see the road, he will be unable to take any avoiding action in case of emergency—and to know that a sleeping passenger is firmly secured also helps the driver's peace of mind greatly.

In competition cars—closed or open—the case in favour of seat belts is much less obvious. Such cars are usually so lightly built that they cannot be expected to resist a severe blow, particularly as an accident is most likely to happen at high speed. In an open car, even if it is fitted with a roll bar, it seems that the driver stands a better chance of escaping severe injury if he is thrown clear of the vehicle than if he remains trapped in it. This is not everybody's view, however, and the American racing rules, amongst others, specify seat belts, even for open racing cars, and the scrutineers will not pass a vehicle if it is not so equipped.

In closed cars built primarily for competition work, the body structure is usually too lightly built to stand up to a roll-over, so that the doors will usually fly open and there is also a good possibility of the driver being ejected, which is all the better, as the roof is bound to collapse under the impact. This can be prevented by reinforcing it with strong tubular roll bar, welded to the chassis structure and following the contour of the roof, just behind the seats. It will obviously add some weight, but the increased safety provided merits due consideration. If such a reinforcement bar is fitted, it is inside the car that the driver will get best protection, and a safety belt will keep him in his seat, even if the doors fly open in the course of an accident.

CHAPTER VIII

TWO HOURS TO GO

IT'S race day. Even for the most experienced racing driver, it is almost impossible not to feel a bit nervous when an important race lies ahead. If he did not, he could only be accused of lack of interest or lack of imagination. Though the reasons for this nervousness are difficult to analyse, it seems certain that fear caused by the risk involved in every high-speed motoring competition must play an important part. As far as I am concerned, I have always found myself much more nervous before a race in which I stood a good chance of success, than where it was obvious from the start that I would be unable to graduate out of the ranks of the also-rans. This is quite understandable, because when victory seems to be within reach, one is usually prepared to take more risks to secure it, not to mention the greater disappointment that failure will cause. But I have also found that somehow my nervousness could be traced to the fear of making a mess of the start. I always used to be much more nervous before a short race, where a good start is vitally important, than before a long one: for some reason Le Mans starts have always been much kinder on my nerves than massed starts with the engine running, and even very important long-distance races made me hardly nervous at all if it had been decided that the burden of starting would be carried by my co-driver.

The biggest trouble is that when you are a member of a well-organised team, there is absolutely nothing you can do to distract your attention from the race before it starts. Your main pre-occupation then is to try and find out if it is going to rain or be fine, whether it is going to be cold or very hot, what sort of tyres—fine-weather or rain tyres—to use, or what your race tactics should be.

Choice of Race Wear

These are not idle thoughts though, and the question of race wear is a particularly important one. The cockpit of a racing car is always a very hot place—even when the car is a rear-engined one a lot of heat is carried into the cockpit from the front radiator and radiated by the pipes running through the cockpit. The only exception among modern racing cars is the Porsche which has a rear-mounted air-cooled engine. Even where the cockpit is open, modern wrap-round windscreens are so efficient that the draught cannot be relied upon to carry the heat away. This, and the fact that after some time the driver warms up to his job, means that after considering the prevalent weather conditions, one's choice of dress for the race usually turns out to be too warm. So the rule should be always to dress as lightly as can reasonably be thought possible. In most cases when the weather is fine, light cotton trousers and a light, short-sleeved shirt will be the most comfortable race wear. It is certainly a good safety measure to have these impregnated for fireproofing and some drivers even rule out short sleeves on the grounds that they give insufficient protection against fire. Nylon is particularly dangerous in case of fire and should never be used for any racing wear or underwear; even the socks should be wool or cotton. On the same grounds, and also because of the increased danger of burns in case the pipe leading to the oil-pressure gauge should break, shorts cannot be recommended, tempting as they may be, except for saloon-car racing where this danger hardly exists. Another safety measure against fire is to rule out one-piece overalls because in a case of emergency, these are much harder to remove than two-piece gear.

Tyre companies such as Dunlop, Avon and Pirelli produce perfectly waterproof two-piece rubber overalls. They should not be worn directly over the bare skin however, as water will always manage to seep in, if only around the neck, and will create a most unwelcome sensation of humidity and cold. Being more or less airtight as well as waterproof, these overalls are extremely hot when it is not raining and my personal opinion is that unless it is almost certain to be raining during the race, it is preferable not to wear them and take a chance on being drenched. Unless it rains very hard, the wrap-round windscreen of a modern single-seater racing car is so efficient that the driver hardly gets wet at all, though it may be useful to wear the rubber trousers, for protection against the water that splashes up through the joints of the body floor.

If the weather is uncertain, the question of whether to use goggles or a visor will also arise. In fine weather, I strongly favour goggles because they cause less distortion, and any dirt that may deposit itself on the lenses, being nearer the eyes than on a visor, is more out of focus and less disturbing. During most of my racing career, I have used rubber-framed flexible goggles, mainly because they are unbreakable and afford an excellent wide field of vision. They are certainly more liable to scratching than goggles made of unbreakable glass, but being cheap they can be replaced frequently.

In rain, all goggles will mist up unless they have previously been treated with some anti-mist compound that is applied to the inside of the lenses. But even then, they will not resist more than about fifteen minutes of rain. If no anti-mist compound is available, a trace of soap applied to the inside of the dry lenses and rubbed clear with a rag will do the trick just as well as most anti-mist compounds.

If heavy rain is anticipated, a visor will have to be used, and even this should be treated against misting (58). Some drivers favour a visor even in fine weather because goggles can give rise to perspiration and even irritation around the frame. But the wind will usually cause the visor to vibrate slightly and thus blur the vision, spoiling its accuracy, and in a front-engined car it is also likely to catch the fumes, sometimes to the extent of incommoding the driver.

If extremely hot weather rather than rain is to be expected during the race, measures should be taken to introduce air into the cockpit wherever possible. Slots and openings should be cut in the body, but only a short time before the race: if they are cut earlier, it can almost be guaranteed that the race will be run in a thunderstorm. Some drivers have used the simple expedient of removing complete body panels where this was practicable, to introduce more air into the cockpit; on a fast circuit, however, this may affect the maximum speed of the car, due to the adverse effect upon the streamlining. Cutting down the sides of the wrap-round windscreen to increase the draught has much the same effect.

Gloves must always be worn, as they not only improve the grip on the steering wheel, but also prevent the formation of blisters, especially on the hand that operates the gear change. Even if the change appears to be quite smooth, the skin of the hand will hardly resist the strain of the 1,500 to 5,000 operations of the gear lever that are necessary in 'around the houses' races like the

Monte Carlo or the Pau Grands Prix, or in a long-distance event like the Le Mans 24 hours race or the Nürburgring 1,000 kilometre race.

In hot weather, the best gloves are those of which the back part is well aerated by large holes or wide-mesh webbing, while chamois leather gloves are very useful in rain, as they facilitate wiping water off the goggles or the visor. Alternatively, a piece of chamois leather may be sewn on the back of the glove, and it is always a good precaution to have a bigger chamois leather handy in a small box where it can be reached easily and where it is sheltered from oil, dust and grit. But make sure that this leather is firmly secured to the car by a piece of string, otherwise, the wind is quite likely to blow it away at the first chance.

Choice of Tyres

Another decision that will have to be taken which depends on the weather is whether to use normal or rain tyres.

Rain tyres have a higher rate of wear, usually a slightly greater rolling resistance and may slightly upset the handling of the car if they are used on dry roads. They should therefore be tried in practice in the dry for a few laps, on a circuit on which they might be used, to enable the driver better to appreciate the pros and cons, in case the weather conditions turn out better than expected during the race.

If you are a member of an organised team, this will probably be the last decision you will have to take before the start of the race. However, if you have a reliable and enthusiastic friend who knows something about motor racing and who can use a stop watch properly, he may be quite useful for some private signalling. If you do not happen to be the star of the team, team managers are apt to neglect you somewhat and signal you rather casually and at long intervals. They may also deliberately give false information, for instance signal a very good lap time, say three or four seconds faster than you are actually doing because for some reason they want you to go even slower; or they may signal a rather indifferent time, making signs to go faster, if they want you to go quicker while you are already doing your best. I have always preferred to know the truth and to be precisely informed of what is happening behind me and in front of me, in order to be my own judge of what to do—even within the frame of team orders—instead of being instructed to go faster or slower without knowing the exact reason why. This friend should settle down somewhere far away from the pits (because team managers usually do not like this sort of private signalling) and at a point where the cars come out of a slow corner so that there is plenty of time for the driver to see the signals. Another wise precaution is to give him a note stating your blood group and rhesus and make sure that he puts it into his briefcase, so he has it handy in case you have a bad accident. This is information which the team manager should also have and, as a further precaution, you may also write it down on your competition licence.

The pre-race interval may well be used for quickly going through the main points of the rules again. All races are of course run according to the same general pattern laid down by the F.I.A. for each particular kind of event. In most cases, however, there are a few 'local' rules which should be known by the driver and the pit staff. For instance: is it permissible to push start the car after a pit stop? Is one allowed to call upon the help of marshals to put the car back on to the road or to restart a stalled engine if one has made a mistake out on the course? May one stop at the pits and restart without stopping the engine? How many people are allowed to work on the car while it is stopped at the pits? In some races, especially long-distance races such as the Le Mans 24 hours race, the rules are so complicated that they must be studied very carefully and a long time in advance; they should be thoroughly understood by the driver as well as by the pit personnel, as any mistake may bring about immediate disqualification.

*   *   *

If you race privately rather than for a team, the question of how to spend the time before the start will hardly arise. The car may have to pass scrutiny again and to be weighed-in between certain hours stated in the rules. After this it will have to be filled with the correct amount of fuel. Measurements during practice will have shown how much fuel is likely to be used during the race. When the tanks are filled, a safety margin of two or three gallons should be allowed, but no more as this will increase the weight of the car unnecessarily. Oil and water levels should be checked once again, tyre pressures should be adjusted and the wheel securing nuts rechecked for tightness. Half an hour before the start, the engine will have to be warmed up, which will possibly necessitate the fitting of special soft plugs which will have to be replaced with the proper racing plugs once it is warm. The plugs to be fitted for the race should have been tried for a few laps during practice, to make sure they are not defective, but otherwise they should be new.

Meanwhile the pit will have to be organised. For a short race very few tools and spare parts will be needed as any important repair will put the car hopelessly out of the picture. The material should include a churn of water, a gallon of oil, a set of spanners, pliers, adjustable spanners, screwdrivers and so on; iron wire and insulating tape should not be forgotten, there should be a set of sparking plugs, a racing jack, a wheel brace and, if possible, one spare front and one spare rear wheel, with tyres. If in spite of uncertain weather you have decided to start with goggles, the visor should be kept in the pit, ready to be fitted over the helmet by someone who knows exactly how to do it and who will have been given the assignment prior to the start.

The most important task of the pit personnel, however, is to keep an exact record of the position of your car in the race and signal you accordingly. Therefore it is necessary to enrol the services of three reliable persons: one lap chart keeper, one time-keeper and one who will give you the signals. If possible, this team should always consist of the same three people who should go to many races and work together. Chart keeping calls for much self-discipline and concentration. Whatever excitement may happen in the race or in the pit area, the person who has accepted the responsibility of keeping the chart must stick to the job, because an inaccurate chart is just as useless as no chart at all. At least during the first few laps, the chart keeper should have a helper who shouts the numbers of the cars as they pass the pits; it is nearly impossible, especially on a short circuit, for the chart keeper to read the numbers of the cars and write them down on the chart simultaneously.

Time-keeping and Signals

The time-keeper must have at least two stop watches—one with two fingers, one of which may be stopped at will—or three stop watches with one finger only. Two of these, or the one with two fingers, will be used to time every single lap completed by the car. The other stop watch is used to measure the gap between your car and the cars directly in front or behind. A further stop

44 Two-finger chronograph: one finger shows the elapsed time; the other can be stopped at any given moment and catches the main finger as soon as it is released. The exact time of passage of several cars can be noted in quick succession and their lap times calculated

45 Timing Board: three stop-watches are operated simultaneously by one single trigger. Their setting is such that one stops, one returns to zero and the third is started by the trigger. The lap time of a given car can thus be read directly every lap, without any risk of a mistake. The operating lever also works a lap counter

46 A vital instrument for rally drivers—the Halda 'Speedpilot'. The hand of the dial on the left is set on the required average speed. At the start of the journey, the 'clock' is zeroed. From then on, the difference between the time shown by the main finger and the time shown by the smaller finger of the right-hand dial will show how many minutes the car is ahead or behind schedule

47 Excessive oil drag in the engine and transmission slow a car until the proper working temperature is reached. Here the rear wheels of a Formula 1 Cooper-Climax V-8 are jacked up while Bruce McLaren warms up the engine and transmission unit, with a gear engaged, before a race. In this picture, the alternative fulcrum points and the adjustable ball sockets of the suspension wishbones can be seen. They allow the suspension geometry, which governs the handling characteristics of the car, to be altered very quickly

48 Cockpit of a 1960 Lotus racing car: the three most important instruments are directly in front of the driver. They are the revolution counter, which features a 'spy' needle, showing the highest figure reached during the race; the oil pressure gauge (left) and the water thermometer (right). At the extreme left, the fuel pressure gauge and two oil temperature gauges can be seen. Note the two foam rubber knee-rests on either side of the scuttle structure

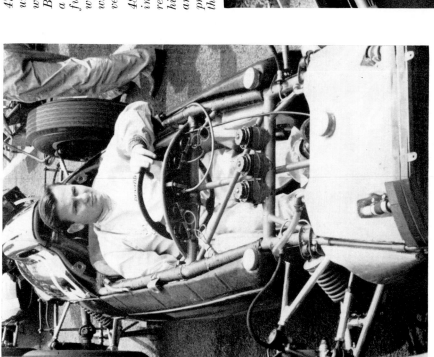

watch, or another with two fingers, will enable him to get both answers on the same lap (*44, 45*).

These intervals may seem much more important than the actual lap times, but this is hardly so. Knowing the times which have been achieved during practice, the lap times put up by the car in the race will enable the pit staff to judge if the driver is really trying, or if he may be expected to go appreciably faster yet. The elapsed time will also show when the car may be expected in the pit area, so that any signals necessary can be shown at the correct moment (*50*). This is particularly important during the night hours of a long-distance race, when it is extremely difficult to identify the cars as they approach.

Signalling should be done with figures and letters which are as large as possible, especially when the pit area is situated at a point where the cars reach a very high speed. It is quite a problem for a driver speeding past the pits at perhaps 130 or 140 m.p.h. readily to identify his signal, which should therefore be made as recognisable as possible or be given by a person wearing clothing of a bright and easily identifiable colour. It is absolutely essential that the signals are given at a point where the driver can devote his attention to them without danger. They must never be given in a zone in which the driver must pick his line for a bend that lies ahead or in a braking area. I once crashed a car in practice before a race, because on their own initiative, my pit attendants had elected to give me signals from the pit nearest to their van, which lay just about where I had to start setting the car for the following bend; my attention was retained a little too long by the sign—which brought me off my line—and I could not avoid crashing. Where the pit is badly situated for signalling, you should try to arrange to have another signalling post in a more convenient place. The best spot is the exit from a hairpin bend, before the cars have had time to regain speed.

If he is to go really fast, a racing driver must entirely concentrate on his driving. Therefore the signals must be as simple and readily understandable as possible. For instance, a driver is not interested in the number of laps he has already completed in the race; what he wants to know is the number of laps to go. So if he is driving in a 50-lap race and has just completed for instance his 38th lap, the sign to be shown is not L38, which would force him to calculate himself that he must do another 12 laps, but L12.

The four main items the driver is interested in are:

(*a*) His position.
(*b*) His distance to the man in front.
(*c*) His lead on the man behind.
(*d*) The number of laps left to be completed.

In some cases, he will also like to know his lap time and to be told of any lap record achieved by himself or another driver. He should also be informed if any of his more dangerous rivals have fallen out of the race.

The first information that should be given is the position. On a short circuit, there is no point in giving this information before the various cars have more or less settled down into their respective positions, that is, after the completion of the third or fourth lap. On a long circuit, however, such as the Nürburgring, this information should already be given at the end of the second lap. Subsequently any change in position should be signalled at once because that is what the driver is most interested in. If the car immediately in front of yours has run away enough to be out of sight, the gap between that car and yours should be given for two consecutive laps, so that you can see at what rate you are losing ground. If the pit manager thinks that, on the grounds of your practice times, you could do better than you actually are doing he might put out a sign giving you your actual lap time. The driver knows best under which circumstances he achieved his best practice laps and he will then be able to judge if he can safely go any faster. There is no point in showing lap times if the track is wet, however, as they lack any basis of comparison.

The driver is also interested to know which is the car in front of his. So instead of showing a board reading '−10', which would mean that he is running 10 seconds behind the car in front, the name of the driver handling that car should be added, to read for instance, '−10 Gurney'. This will help him in his judgement, as previous racing experience or practice will have shown if he can hope to match that particular combination of car and driver or not. If the driver sees that he cannot close the gap between the car in front and his, or if he is out in front of everyone else, he will be more interested in knowing which, and how far, is the next car behind him. Time and again, for instance every five laps, the number of laps left to be run must also be signalled. If, driving as fast as you can, you are closing up at the rate of 1 second a lap

98

"G. P." LAP CHART

Date_____

Circuit_____ Length_____ Air Temp. _____ Existing Lap Record_____

Event_____ Weather_____ by_____

Car_____ No. _____ Tyre Pressure. Front _____ Fastest practice time_____

1st Driver_____ Rear _____

2nd Driver_____ Axle Ratio _____ by_____

CAR NO.	DRIVERS	POSITION	NUMBER OF LAPS																							
			1	2	3	4	5	6	7	8	9	10	11	12	13	14	15	16	17	18	19	20	21	22	23	24	25
		1																									
		2																									
		3																									
		4																									
		5																									
		6																									
		7																									
		8																									
		9																									
		10																									
		11																									
		12																									
		13																									
		14																									

POSITION	26	27	28	29	30	31	32	33	34	35	36	37	38	39	40	41	42	43	44	45	46	47	48	49	50	51	52	53	54	55	56
1																															
2																															
3																															
4																															
5																															
6																															
7																															
8																															
9																															
10																															
11																															
12																															
13																															
14																															

RACE RESULT:

1st_____

2nd_____

3rd_____

REMARKS:

Figure 49

99

ASTON MARTIN RACING TIME SHEET.

SHEET No.

EVENT: 1,000 Km. Race   CIRCUIT: Nurburgring   DATE: Sunday, 1st June, 1958.

CAR: CHASSIS NO.: DBR1/3
ENGINE NO.: RB6.300/3

GEAR BOX NO.:
AXLE RATIO: 3.62/1 ЗН

SPECIAL DETAILS: Red Ident.   No: 1   MECHANIC - HONES
Circuit length 14.2 miles

DRIVER(S) MOSS/BRABHAM

Gillian Harris

LAP	PLAN	ELAPSED TIME	UNIT LAP TIME	EARLY OR LATE	REMARKS	BAR:	TEMP: 59°F	Hg.:
				Hot, sunny				
1			10-02.4		MOSS SIGNAL 1 LAP	FUEL 130 litres 6.50x16R 6.00x16F	35F/38R	I
2		19-51	9-48.6		SIGNAL +12 MOS, HAW			I
3		29-34.6	9-43.6		SIGNAL +15 MOS, HAW, 3 LAP			I
4		39-17	9-42.4		SIGNAL +21 MOS, HAW (somehing dragging under car)			I
5		49-06.4	9-49.4		SIGNAL +28 MOS, HAW (bent to gearbox bottomed)	+39		I
6		58-58.2	9-51.8		SIGNAL +38 MOS, HAW, 6 LAP	+38		I
7		68-45.4	9-47.2		SIGNAL +38 SAL. OUT	+44		I
8		78-34	9-48.6		SIGNAL +44 LAP 8	+46		I
9		88-18.6	9-44.6		SIGNAL 1 LAP → (4'6" RAO)	+53		I
10		98-08.6	9-50 06.8	IN PIT STOP	Change drivers Car sliding, 3rd gear jumping out			I
11		108-42.4	10-27		BRABHAM SIGNAL +41 BRAB, HAW (Haw passed just beyond pit)			I
12		118-59.4	10-17		SIGNAL 1 LAP → (HAW in lead; BRA -32)			I
13		129-21.4	10-22 1-21	IN PIT STOP	Change Driver Fuel (Gearbox OK) Tyres ALL 4 changed ½ gall oil 12			
14		140-42	9-59.6		MOSS (Seltan in)			I
15		150-37	9.55		SIGNAL 1' MOSS, COL	+31		
16		160-35	9-58		SIGNAL +41" MOSS COLL			I
17	2L 50'27.2"	170-27.2	9-52.2		SIGNAL +52" MOS COL	+1'12.8"		
18	3L 00:28.2"	180-28.2	10-01	MASTER 3L 00:23.4	SIGNAL +73" MOS, COL LAP 18	+80'		
19		190-17.2	9-49		SIGNAL +80" MOS, COL			
20		200-12	9-54.8		SIGNAL +96" MOS, COL	+1m44"		I
21		210-01.8	9-49.8		SIGNAL +104" MOS, COL	+115"		I
22		219-54	9-52.2		SIGNAL +115 MOS, COL LAP 22	+134"		I
23		229-47	9-53		SIGNAL 1 LAP →	2m31"		
24		239-43.4	9-56.4 07.8	IN PIT STOP	Change Driver Slipping out of 3rd Oil on circuit Oil down to 45 min minutes			
25		240-27.6	10-36.4		BRABHAM SIGNAL +155" BRA, COL	Tem 70°F		
26		250-47.	10-20.2		SIGNAL +123 BRA, COL	+106"		I
27		261-06.4	10-19.4		SIGNAL +106 BRA, COL	+90"		I
28		271-32.4	10-26		SIGNAL 1 LAP →	+64"		
29		288-07.4	10-35	IN PIT STOP	Change Driver Change tyres Rear only oil 1½ gall FUEL			
30		292-23.	1-08 10-07.6		MOSS SIGNAL +71 MOS, HAW	+81		

50   *Timing chart for the Moss/Brabham Aston Martin*

100

ASTON MARTIN RACING TIME SHEET.

EVENT:................................... CIRCUIT:......................... DATE:....................

CAR: CHASSIS NO.:...DBR1/3............ GEAR BOX NO.:.....................
ENGINE NO.:...RB 6 300/3........... AXLE RATIO.:......................

SPECIAL DETAILS.......................... CAR NO: I

DRIVER(S)....................................

LAP	PLAN	ELAPSED TIME	UNIT LAP TIME	EARLY OR LATE	REMARKS	BAR:	TEMP:	Hg.:
13 31		302-21·4	9-58·4		SIGNAL +81 MOS, HAW			I
12 32		312-20	9-58·6		SIGNAL +90 O.K		-99"	! I
11 33		322-17·2	9-57·2		SIGNAL +99 HAW, LAP 33 (HAW SPUN)		+2·42"	I
10 34		332-15·6	9-58·4		SIGNAL +262 HAW		+4'11"	I
9 35		342-20·4	10-04·8		SIGNAL +251 HAW		+252"	I
8 36		352-19·4	9-59		SIGNAL +252 HAW LAP 36		+4'17"	I
7 37		362-19·4	10-00		SIGNAL +257 HAW, LAP 37	Lapped Brooks		I
6 38		372-19·4	10-00		SIGNAL +257 HAW, LAP 38			
5 39		382-19·4	10-00		SIGNAL +257 HAW, LAP 39			
4 40		392-19·4	10-00		SIGNAL +253 HAW, LAP 40			
3 41		402-23·4	10-04		SIGNAL +250 HAW LAP 41			
2 42		412-31·4	10-08		SIGNAL +243 HAW LAP 42			
1 43		422-37·6	10-06·2		SIGNAL 1 LAP			
44	7hr 12m 49.6s	432-49·6	10-12		1st			
					maxi 6,100			

99·6
·21
11 20·6
127 21·4
140 42·0

97 08·6
10-33·8
108 42·4

DBR1/300 in the 1958 Nürburgring 1,000 kilometres race

on an opponent who has a 30 seconds lead and there are still 30 laps to go, your race tactics will obviously be very different from what they would be if only 7 or 8 laps were left to be done. With no hope of catching your rival before the end, you would then concentrate on keeping your position while nursing the car as much as possible.

Signalling is quite a difficult task because it is not easy for the person in charge of it to know exactly what the driver wants to know at any given moment. So a code should be decided upon by which the driver can ask his pit for the information he is most likely to want. It may be decided that if the driver points forward with his finger, he wants to know how far ahead is the car in front of him; pointing rearward will then mean, 'By how much am I leading the next man?' Turning circles with his finger may be the code for asking how many laps are left to be run, while tapping with a hand on the helmet is the usual sign for informing the pit staff that the driver intends to come into the pits on the following lap, and everything likely to be needed, such as oil, water, fuel, the jack and the more usual tools, should be kept ready.

Most pit managers usually concentrate so much on their own car and the ones immediately in front and behind, that they tend to forget about the general pattern of the race. Here is an example: your car is running, say, in fourth or fifth position, without being seriously challenged. Suddenly one of the leaders makes a short pit stop and rejoins the race three or four positions behind your car and, say, 45 seconds behind on time. This combination of a fast car and fast driver will now probably start lapping very quickly in an endeavour to make up as many places as possible before the end of the race. A good pit manager will immediately become aware of this menace and signal for instance '+45 Moss'; on the next lap, the signal may become '+42 Moss' and the next time round '+39 Moss', thus disregarding all the cars that might find themselves between yours and that of the driver who is coming up fast through the field. Having been informed of the danger in time, you may be able to find just that little extra speed that will reduce the average rate at which your dangerous rival is closing the gap from 3 to 2 seconds and thus keep him at bay until the end of the race. If, using less foresight, your pit manager had waited until this faster driver had come up through the field to occupy the position just behind you before warning you of his presence—when he had closed up to say, 10 seconds—it would probably have been too late for you to take any counter-measures.

Though I believe that, in normal circumstances, the pit signals should give the driver information rather than orders, this is a case where the pit manager should even take the initiative of putting out a faster sign as soon as he has realised the menace, in order to enable his driver to react immediately. But in the following laps, the signals should make it quite clear why the faster signal has been given.

It is useful for the pit manager to know if the driver has actually understood the signal put out to him. As far as possible all signals which have been understood should be acknowledged by a sign. Signals may be missed by a driver because of bad visibility, or because the signal is hidden by another car which is just being passed. The signalling personnel should be aware of such a possibility and should not hesitate, if necessary, to repeat the signal on the next lap if they believe that it has not been clearly understood. In a long-distance race, it is of particular importance that the signal calling the driver in for refuelling is not missed. Many races have been won by stretching the distance between refuelling stops to the utmost, thus saving one stop compared with rival competitors. But this also means that there are only a few drops of fuel left in the tank when the car comes in for refuelling and if the driver misses the 'come-in' signal, his car is in danger of running out of fuel and being put out of the race. It is therefore a wise precautionary measure to signal the refuelling stop twice: two laps before the car is due in, a signal should be put out 'In 2 laps'; next time round, the signal should read 'In' so that if the driver misses one of the signals, he still knows exactly when to stop.

When night driving is involved, such as at Le Mans, in the Rheims 12 hours race, or in some of the races included in the Tour de France, it is essential that the signalling panel should be properly illuminated and also be made readily recognisable by a particular colour or a large-sized sign attached to it. The normal lighting of the pit area is quite insufficient to enable the driver readily to pick out his own signal from the maze of boards being kept ready to be shown to other cars.

Race Tactics

The famous racing motor cyclist the late Fergus Anderson, who was as brilliant a personality as he was a rider, once wrote that the best racing man was the one who won the races going as slowly as possible. However, this principle which the experienced driver should always bear in mind, hardly applies to the newcomer, who will usually have to struggle very hard to get a decent place, rather than win the race with something in hand. Practice times will usually have given you a rough idea of what you may expect from the race. If your practice times indicate that you have a chance of winning it, it may be well worth your while to go as fast as possible and try to challenge your main opponents right from the start, even if this means taxing the engine to its limit and using the brakes to their maximum. By keeping your opponents busy, you may tempt them into overstressing their cars or induce them to make a mistake. Then will be the time to drive to the finish as safely as possible.

On a difficult circuit, a difference in the lap times of two drivers may possibly only reflect the lesser knowledge of the course of one of them who, given more practice, could do better. If it is felt that this may be the case for a potentially dangerous opponent, the obvious thing to do is again to go as fast as possible right from the start so as to build up a useful lead before the opposition, getting a better knowledge of the circuit with every lap, is able to match your speed. This tactic helped me win many touring and sports car races on the Spa circuit, and also to obtain better places in Formula I races than I would probably have managed when matched against the same professional Grand Prix drivers on other tracks.

Unfortunately one does not always have a car that is a match for the opposition but even then, and perhaps more than ever, careful planning may pay dividends. On a fast circuit incorporating long straights, you may decide to try to 'get a tow' from the slipstream of faster cars. This will only succeed if the car you want to follow is not more than eight to ten miles an hour faster than your own. Within this speed range, slipstreaming may push up your speed to lap times which it would be impossible for your car to achieve without outside help. The increase in speed due to slipstreaming will also inevitably result in increased engine revolutions per minute, so that if your car is correctly geared to reach the highest possible maximum speed on the straight when it is driven on its own, the gain in speed due to slipstreaming will send the engine speed 300 or 400 revs above the permissible limit. In the long run, this is bound to spell trouble and if you feel that you

51 However quickly the author managed to jump out of his Ferrari for the last pit stop before driving on to win the 1960 Le Mans race, a mechanic has already opened the tank filler cap and is just about to push in the nozzle of the pressurized refuelling system

52 Every second lost in the pits must be made up by the driver on the road, at great risk to himself and his car. Attention to details can often save precious seconds. Here a mechanic uses a huge syringe to force oil into the reservoir of the dry sump lubrication system of the DB3S Aston Martin, which the late Peter Collins and the author drove into second place in the tragic 1955 Le Mans 24 Hours Race

53 *The cars have just moved away from a massed start, where they were lined up in groups of three, two, three, etc. Already the cars from the second row have drawn almost level with those which started from the first*

54 *This is what can easily happen if a driver is too keen to get off to a good start, or if a car fails to move at the fall of the flag. The drivers involved are the late Ron Flockhart jumping Jack Lewis' Cooper*

can rely on 'getting a tow' regularly from other cars during the race, it may be useful to gear higher accordingly.

Slipstreaming nowadays pays off much more in Gran Turismo and sports car racing than in Formula I racing where the cars have become so small that their slipstream is almost negligible. In long-distance races, slipstreaming may be used not to increase the car's maximum speed, but to save the engine and, above all, to reduce fuel consumption. Following a vehicle of equal performance, your car will go as fast as it would go on its own while using about only two-thirds of the maximum throttle opening, and this may enable you to do two or three more laps on a tankful, which may save you one refuelling stop in the end.

Even if you are unlucky enough to be driving a car which is completely outclassed, intelligent tactics may bring returns. In a long race, there is always a chance that faster cars will fall out, thus enabling you to get a decent place if your car is driven with this possibility in mind, and treated in such a manner that it stands a good chance of finishing.

If on the other hand, you know your car to be unreliable, even if it is nursed as much as possible in racing, the better scheme is probably to go as fast as you can for as long as it holds together, in order to put up a decent show while you *are* in the race. If you do this for a few races, you may hope that someone will notice your performance and offer you a drive in a better car when the occasion arises.

CHAPTER IX

THE RACE

THE pit organisation having been laid down, all arrangements having been made for accurate timing and signalling, and the race tactics having been decided upon, you can now concentrate on making a good start.

There are two main types of start: one is the so-called Le Mans start (*55*), which is often used in Gran Turismo and sports car races though no longer in Britain; the other is the Grand Prix start (*53*).

The Le Mans Start

For the Le Mans start, the cars are all lined up, herringbone fashion, with their backs to the pits. The rule is that the engine must be stopped and the doors must be closed. About one minute before the start, the drivers take position in a circle painted on the road, opposite their respective cars. At the starter's signal, everyone runs across the road, jumps into his car and tries to get away as quickly as he can. The goggles should have been properly adjusted about ten seconds before the flag is due to be dropped, but no more, to obviate misting up. Obviously the gear lever should have been left in first gear, so that the only thing the driver has to do, as soon as he has got into his seat, is to depress the clutch pedal, operate the starter and release the clutch as soon as the engine has fired, to get the car off the mark. A combined ignition and starter switch saves valuable time, but if this is not provided, and the car's fuel system incorporates an electric pump that is brought into action by the same switch as the ignition, this should not be left on while the driver is waiting for the flag to fall, because the pump may flood the carburettors and make the engine reluctant to start.

All this sounds very simple, but it is amazing how much time can be saved at the start if the starting procedure is thoroughly rehearsed before the race. Careful timing will show if, with an open car, time is saved by jumping over the door into the cockpit rather than opening the door. Every movement should be studied so that the driver is correctly seated as quickly as possible, and no time is lost in locating the ignition and starter switches. Drivers who jump into their cars without proper rehearsal have found themselves sitting with one leg going through the steering wheel—hardly the right way of making a fast getaway! And remember that if you do use the door, you can save the time taken to close it, because it will automatically slam itself shut as soon as the car accelerates away.

Of course the most brilliantly performed starting procedure can be marred by an engine that is reluctant to fire. It is therefore absolutely essential to find out the exact throttle opening on which the engine, that has been previously warmed up, starts most readily. And it is equally important that in the excitement of the actual start of the race, the driver keeps his head and strictly adheres to the drill that has been found to give the best results. Sports and Gran Turismo car races for which the Le Mans starting procedure is often used, are usually quite crowded; cars of all capacities run together and a messed-up start may not only mean the loss of a good starting position, but also that one may have to wind one's way through a compact field of slower cars which will delay one's progress while the leaders consolidate their positions.

The Grand Prix Start

For a Grand Prix start the cars are lined up in staggered rows with three cars in the front row, two cars in the second, three cars in the third, and so on. There may of course be more cars per row if the road is wide enough. The positions are usually determined by practice times, the drivers who have put up the best times getting a place in the front row, the next best in the second row and so forth. In most cases, the fastest driver in any given row is placed in the position that will give the inside of the first bend or corner after the start, so as to minimise any possible baulking.

About three minutes before the starting signal is due to be given, all cars should be in position on the starting grid. Between two minutes and one minute to go, the engine, which will have been previously warmed up so that the oil and coolant will have

109

reached their proper working temperatures, should be started. If it is started up earlier (which is usually forbidden by the regulations anyway), it is bound to overheat unduly (unless it is air-cooled), as racing cars do not have a fan to activate the air circulation through the radiator. As soon as the engine is running, give a glance at the instruments to check if everything is working properly. The idling speed should be kept between 3,000 and 4,000 r.p.m. to prevent plug fouling.

If, for any reason, the engine should not start, let everyone know by holding an arm up in the air. This is particularly important, as the other drivers must be informed that you will be unable to move when the starting signal is given, so that they can act accordingly—otherwise a bad mix-up is very likely to happen (53). According to the current rules, a car is not allowed to start in a race unless the engine has been started up by the self-starter.

If all goes well, everything should be ready when the sign 'one minute to go' appears, while you sit as calmly as possible in the cockpit, watching the instruments and the other cars. Not until the half-minute sign comes up should you adjust your goggles, as otherwise they may mist up, especially if the weather is cool. Only when this has been done should first gear be engaged, as due to the high idling speed of the engine, considerable stress is imposed upon the clutch-release bearing if the clutch is kept disengaged for any length of time. With the start now in sight, the engine speed must be increased to the figure which experience has proved to give the best getaway, which probably lies between 4,000 and 5,500 r.p.m.; the clutch is slowly released to the point where you feel it is just beginning to grip. In order to prevent the car from starting to creep (which may involve a time penalty) you may slightly apply the foot brake by using the heel-and-toe method, or use the hand brake, but a small block of wood, or a stone, about half an inch high, placed in front of a wheel when the car is pushed to the start, provides a much more convenient way of preventing the car from rolling forward too soon.

Down goes the flag and in goes the clutch! This is the moment where very delicate control of the pedals is essential. Clutch slip and wheelspin should keep the engine running fast enough to provide useful power, but excessive wheelspin will mar the start and excessive clutch slip may burn the clutch. Burnt clutches have lost many races within five seconds of the start.

Even the best of drivers can make a mess of the start. In 1959, when he looked a probable World Champion, Tony Brooks lost all chance of the title when he burnt his clutch on the starting line of the Italian Grand Prix at Monza, in trying to make a lightning getaway. Moss himself has been seen to be left behind on the starting line and quite often back markers who are less in the limelight than front-row starters manage to jump the flag and wind their way through the field to join the leaders. If this happens to you, it gives you a good chance to learn something and also to take advantage of the faster cars' slipstream; but be fair and do not forget to look in your mirror. Faster cars and drivers will soon come up behind you; they have proved during practice that they can lap faster than you can, so there is no point in baulking them and jeopardising their chances of catching up with the better starters. Don't make a nuisance of yourself—let them by as soon as they come up close enough and you see a chance to give way to them. By trying to stay in front of them, you only ruin their chances in the race without any benefit to yourself; on the contrary you will probably get rather nervous and sooner or later make a mistake. But when you have let a faster man pass you, by all means try and stay with him; observe his methods, watch where he brakes and see where his line is different from yours: you will probably finish the race a better driver.

It is also very easy to over-rev the engine during the first few hundred yards following the start. At this stage the cars are proceeding in such close company that but little attention can be devoted to the instruments in general and the rev-counter in particular, while the noise level is so high that it is almost impossible to distinguish the roar of one's own engine from that produced by the other cars. This is why it is not unusual for an excellently prepared car to be retired on the very first lap, due to a bent valve. Such a mistake has occasionally been the lot of even some of the very best drivers, but it is still no excuse for not being extremely careful that it does not happen to you.

In the Race

Apart from trying to save split seconds everywhere he can, of which enough has been said in previous chapters, one of the driver's main problems during the race will have to be faced when other competitors must be overtaken or when a faster car comes up behind.

When two cars and drivers are very nearly equally matched,

and are racing neck and neck, there is, of course, no question of the one in front giving way to the other, but it is the duty of the leader to make room for his follower to pass, if he can, whenever it does not bring him off his proper line. For the follower, the only chances to get by his rival are to out-brake him into a corner, to pass him after the corner if he has managed to take the latter a little faster, or by slipstreaming on a straight.

These cases have been dealt with in Chapter V. The drivers involved in a struggle of this sort always use their mirrors extensively to watch their opponent and know exactly what he is about to do. It is therefore current practice and perfectly safe for the car behind to try to overtake on either side, whichever is the more convenient and safe, except on a straight, where the car in front should keep sufficiently to its right to enable a slipstreaming driver to pass on the left, if he can.

The problem is quite different when the speed differential of the two cars is greater or the drivers are less evenly matched. A driver who knows that he cannot match some of the other competitors in the race—and he *should* know from experience or practice times—should keep an eye on his mirrors every time a long enough straight between two corners provides the opportunity of doing so, and occasionally cast a quick glance over his shoulder at a hairpin (if there is one on the circuit), the better to judge the distance between himself and the cars that may come up behind. A faster car or driver should never be baulked by one who is definitely slower, and a driver who does not bear this in mind is bound to make himself unpopular very soon.

As soon as a faster car has come up sufficiently close to be expected to pass at the first opportunity, you should give way to enable it to pass as easily as possible, even at the cost of a few fractions of a second if you are not terribly pressed yourself. For instance, if the faster driver is coming up just behind at the approach to a corner, you should start slowing down a little earlier than usual, yield the better approach position to the corner, and make it quite clear that you are prepared to let the other car overtake you, eventually signalling the other driver on which side you are going to make room for him (*56*).

There is, of course, no point in losing time unnecessarily, and if you see that you can take the bend without getting in the other driver's way you should do so, and make room at the exit of the curve. If it is a right-hand corner which, following the normal line, you will leave close to the left-hand side of the road, you should stay there and signal the driver behind to overtake on the right, and you must not cut across his path again before he can do so.

In races in which cars of vastly different performance run together, as is usual in sports or G.T. car events, overtaking can become a major hazard. Down the long straight at Le Mans, for instance, the speed differential between the fastest and the slowest cars may be as much as 60 or 70 m.p.h., and if one of the slower cars pulls out for overtaking when one of the faster cars comes up behind at full speed, a nasty situation may arise. In this case, the driver of the slower car about to pull out is in a better position to judge the speed of the vehicle coming up behind him, than the driver of the faster vehicle is to judge the relative speed of the two slower cars. This is why the driver of a comparatively slow car, who is about to pull out for overtaking—or maybe only to take his correct line through a corner—should be particularly careful and make quite sure that in doing so he does not cut across the line of a much faster vehicle coming up behind. In any case, the driver of the faster car will be extremely grateful for any signal by the driver of the slower car that will inform him of his intentions. If the slower car is closed, and hand signals are not practicable, the driver may use his direction indicators to show that he is aware of the car coming up, for example by flashing his right-hand side indicators, to indicate his intention to stay on the right-hand side of the road.

Flag Marshals

Unfortunately not every driver is a perfect gentleman who is prepared to give way to a fellow-competitor as soon as he is obviously in a position to overtake him. Cases of deliberate baulking are fortunately rather rare; they occur more often in second-rate events in which some drivers take part who have no other means of keeping their opponents at bay. Other inferior drivers are kept so busy by holding their car on the road that they don't seem to have any time left for looking in their mirror.

It is for those who never take a look behind that flag marshals, posted along the circuit, have been provided with a blue flag. When it is held still, it just draws the attention of the driver who gets it to the fact that he is being followed by another competitor who may wish to overtake him. If the marshal waves the blue flag, the driver is instructed to make room for a faster competitor who is about to overtake him. A driver who feels that he is being baulked by another competitor may appeal to a flag marshal to use his blue flag by waving his hand to draw his attention to the situation.

The use of the blue flag is a much more difficult task than one might think. If the flag is abused, it loses all significance, and drivers cease to take any notice of it. But it *must* be used when circumstances call for it, otherwise it is just as well to have no flag marshals at all. It is quite difficult for anyone without racing experience to judge when the flag should be given, and when not. A red car is not necessarily faster than the others, and a good flag marshal should not only be fully aware of what is happening in the race, in order to be prepared to show the blue flag at the appropriate moment, but he should also know at first glance who is who and which, of two cars racing in close company, is likely to be the faster one.

Marshals also have other flags at their disposal: the yellow caution flag, the red flag which is very rarely used and calls for a full and immediate stop, and the blue-and-yellow striped oil warning flag. The correct use of the latter also calls for considerable experience, not only in detecting oil left on the track by competing cars, but also in judging if the amount that has been spilled is harmless or warrants the use of the flag. The oil warning flag should be used only in the area made dangerous by the oil, and only for the time necessary for competitors to complete a few laps —just long enough to make sure the drivers remember where the oil is. If it is held out longer than necessary, it will cause confusion and may not be taken seriously if another patch of oil is left on the track at a later stage of the race.

55 Drivers running to their cars for a Le Mans start. As not all drivers and cars get off to an equally good start, this is a good way of partly sorting them out before they reach the first corner but, if the race is of short duration, an engine that is reluctant to start gets very heavily penalized by this procedure

56 Phil Hill signalling to Trevor Taylor that he is making room for him to overtake on his left-hand side. This implies that, if necessary, he will also slow down to make his opponent's task easier. The negative camber used on all wheels of modern racing cars can clearly be seen in this picture

57 Such conditions make high-speed driving almost impossible, as the thick layer of water has no time to escape from under the tyres which eventually completely lose contact with the road (Graham Hill, B.R.M., Brussels, 1962)

58 Oil, dust and water may render the windscreen and the vizor almost completely opaque, but if the vizor is cut to an appropriate depth, the driver is still able to see the road under the vizor and over the screen without suffering too much from wind and rain. (The author driving a Porsche at Le Mans, 1958)

CHAPTER X

DRIVING IN RAIN, WINTER AND AT NIGHT

In the Wet

MOST ordinary drivers are scared of driving on wet roads. It is, however, mostly a question of adaptation, especially in racing where unforeseen obstacles are fewer than on the roads. In racing, when cornering, braking and accelerating, a car is always being driven at the limit of its adhesion. If this is altered by a wet or damp road surface, the driver's judgement will have to be adjusted accordingly. This means that cornering speeds will have to be lower and braking distances increased, while the accelerator and brake pedals must be treated with more delicacy to avoid locking or spinning the wheels, of which the latter will reduce the car's acceleration and produce unwanted power slides of the tail. On the normal kind of circuit, it will even be found that rain does not change the position of braking points before corners as much as would be expected. The reason for this is that, cornering speeds being lower in the wet, cars leave the corners at a slower speed, which slows them all along the following straight, so that they do not reach the next braking area at the same high speed as in the dry. On a slippery road, any unwanted movement of the vehicle, any incipient slide, must be checked with even greater accuracy and rapidity than usual if it is to be controlled at all.

As, basically, the degree of slipperiness of road does not alter the driving technique, it makes very little difference how slippery the road is and whether it is made slippery by water, snow or ice. Fortunately the speeds at which bends and corners can be taken become progressively lower as the road gets more slippery, so that everything happens with the car travelling more slowly. As the road gets more slippery, the difficulty shifts from the curves to the straights. Here the same high speeds are reached as when the

117

road is dry; whereas in curves the speed of the car must be reduced to lessen the forces acting upon the vehicle so that the balance between these forces and the grip of the tyres on the road is maintained. On the straights, only the grip is reduced but not the momentum of the car and the various forces generated by it. On a very slippery surface, such as snow or ice, the point can even be reached where the drag caused by the air and rolling resistance, becomes equal to the tractive force of the driving wheels. This sets a limit to the speed that can be reached by the vehicle under the prevailing conditions. At this speed the entire adhesion of the driving wheels is used for propelling the car; the wheels tend to spin and are unable to oppose any resistance to lateral forces that may act upon the vehicle. The latter thus becomes directionally unstable and can only stay on the road if the driver constantly corrects its direction of progress.

Braking distances are of course increased on slippery roads, making it necessary for the driver to look farther ahead for any possible obstruction. This is important enough on the race track, but it is absolutely vital on the open road, where the sight must be concentrated much further ahead—looking out for a bad corner, for a dangerous crossroad, for oncoming traffic when overtaking or for the odd cyclist. Accurate assessment of how far ahead the eyes must look for any possible danger, in relation to the grip afforded by the road surface, becomes increasingly difficult as the speed rises and calls for considerable experience. Drivers are usually reluctant to look far enough ahead, because the farther they look, the more their attention is distracted from placing the vehicle correctly in relation to its immediate surroundings.

A very heavy downpour however may completely change the driving conditions at high speed and make them extremely dangerous. This happens when the rain comes down at a higher rate than the water is drained from the road surface. The road then becomes coated with a layer of water of measurable thickness; at normal speeds, this water is squished away by the tyre as it rolls along, and what is not deflected to either side of the tyre, finds its way into the grooves of the tread pattern. As the speed increases, however, there is less and less time for the water to escape from under the tyre and a point can be reached where not all the water is squished away in time for the tyre to make contact with the road surface: it becomes buoyant; the car just floats on the water and becomes uncontrollable. In such an event there is very little even the best of drivers can do but hope that the wheels will reach a patch of road where they can regain their grip before it is too late. Harry Schell's fatal accident at Silverstone in 1960 can almost certainly be attributed to a case of this description, which is more likely to present itself on the modern sort of flat and beautifully smooth road surface, on which the water tends to lie, than on a rougher surface (57).

It is sometimes said that there are drivers who like racing in rain. This is yet another example of nonsense being talked about motor racing. No driver actually likes, or ever did like, driving in rain, if only because the best of waterproof overalls are utterly inefficient at keeping out the water that finds its way everywhere into the cockpit of a racing car, making the driver utterly miserable and uncomfortable. And even if, from that point of view, he is lucky enough to be driving a closed car, the reduced visibility makes racing much more dangerous in rain than in fine weather. In open cars, rain blurs the sight through the goggles or the visor, dirt and oil raised by other cars make them become progressively more opaque, goggles and even visors eventually tend to mist up, and other cars raise impenetrable clouds of spray. Following another car in such conditions means driving completely blind and relying entirely on the judgement of the man in front. Any sort of anticipation is ruled out, and if the other driver is himself following a car made almost invisible by its own spray and hiding everything else, the risk of an extremely grave multiple collision cannot be discounted. Conditions are, if anything, even worse when the spray hits the screen of a closed car. The best wipers, which become almost useless anyway at speeds above 110 or 120 m.p.h., are utterly unable to cope with that sort of situation at all, even at 60 m.p.h.

No driver therefore *likes* to race in rain. It is true however that drivers sometimes hope for rain because it will give them a better chance. The more delicate touch that is necessary to get the best results on a slippery track may sort out drivers who on a dry road would be equally matched. Rain can also be an advantage for the car rather than for the driver. Fast and powerful cars are always more handicapped by rain than small cars, as an example will show. Imagine a curve that can be taken at about 130 m.p.h. on a dry road; in rain the speed will have to be reduced to say 110 m.p.h., so that all fast cars will be slowed down by 20 m.p.h. through this curve. A smaller car, which has not enough power to reach more than 100 m.p.h. at this point will, however, not be slowed by the more slippery condition of the road at all; it will take this curve at around 100 m.p.h., whatever the weather and still with a useful safety margin. Rain thus levels out the usable power—which is why the drivers of less powerful cars often wish for rain, even if they don't actually like it.

Winter Driving

There is actually very little difference between driving on a road made slippery by rain and on a road made slippery by snow or ice. Very fortunately, however, racing cars are not as a rule driven over snow-covered or icy roads, where their very high power-to-weight ratio and the lack of flexibility of their engines would make them very difficult to drive. It is true that in some countries in the North, race meetings are held on frozen lakes, but for these occasions the cars are fitted with special tyres on which spikes protrude from the tread and which afford a reasonably good grip.

Rally drivers, on the other hand, are often faced with these sorts of road condition, when driving a touring car at rally speeds with a tight schedule is very similar to driving a racing car on a rain-soaked road and calls for a very similar technique.

In typical winter rallies, like the Monte Carlo Rally, these conditions call for special consideration, the choice of tyres being particularly important. Whenever the schedule leaves a certain margin, snow tyres are best, as they are acceptable on normal dry roads as well as on snow or ice. On clear roads they cut down performance, due to their increased rolling resistance compared with normal tyres, but not to an embarrassing extent, while they afford a notably better grip on snowbound roads.

The problem becomes much more intricate when the rally is essentially in the form of a speed test. If it is known that the roads are covered with deep snow over the entire timed section, which usually is a difficult one which does not permit very high speeds, then the best scheme is probably to fit chains to the driving wheels and snow tyres to the other pair—the old-fashioned chains probably being the most efficient means of getting a good grip on a road covered with deep snow. Where the going is faster, however, and where speeds of over 75 m.p.h. can be reached, or where parts of the section are likely—or known—to be clear of snow, chains must not be used, as they are likely to break up under the strain of the centrifugal force or to cut up the tyres very rapidly. In this case, plain snow tyres probably make the best compromise.

For fast driving under timed, competitive conditions, over icy roads, tyres fitted with tungsten-carbide studs are imperative. Such tyres are produced by some of the usual tyre manufacturers, but the studs can also be fitted to normal, or snow, tyres of any type by specialists.

The studs must not be too long, otherwise they completely upset the handling of the car on the clear sections of road; if they are short, they are not a very great help in deep snow, but they enormously increase the grip of the tyres on roads covered with ice or hard, frozen snow. The best-known and most widely used studs which can be fitted to any type of tyre, are made by the small firm Vaillant, in Cluse, France. The Pirelli BS3 tyre, notable for its interchangeable treads, can also be fitted with a studded tread especially made by the manufacturer.

Whatever type is used, there is no doubt at all that a minimum equipment of six tyres per car is essential for winter rallying: four snow tyres and two studded tyres for fitting to the driving wheels where icy roads are to be expected. Well-organised competitors always arrange for spare tyres, of all the types likely to be needed, to be available at prearranged depots before sections are reached where the type of tyre used may become a decisive factor of success.

Racing at Night

Racing at night is rather a rare occurrence today. Now that the Mille Miglia in its historic form has had to be abandoned, and with the Rheims 12 hours and Goodwood 9 hours races not having been held for some years, the only two events on the international racing calendar in which the headlights must be used are the Sebring 12 hours race and the Le Mans 24 hours Grand Prix d'Endurance. However, much of what is said here about the preparation of a car for night racing also applies to rallies of which— in view of the ever-increasing congestion of the roads—the more exacting stages are now usually covered during the hours of darkness.

First of all—and this is a general rule applying to daylight racing as well as to night racing—the driver should make himself as comfortable as possible. Any bright part that might reflect light, from other cars running behind or from your own, should be painted dull and dark—even if it does not look quite so smart. This means that the whole dash, especially the horizontal part at the base of the windscreen, must be painted black, and so should the instrument bezels, and steering column, the steering-wheel spokes, the rear-view mirror frame and any stay that may be used for holding the windscreen in place, particularly if the car is an open one. In this case, the dull paint will also prevent the reflection of the sun during the bright hours, which can become very tiring for a driver whose nerves have already been strained by several hours of racing or rallying. The absence of reflections in the screen is also a great help in fog.

Even in daylight, it is not an easy task accurately to read the figures on the smaller instruments, such as the oil pressure gauge and the oil and water thermometers. For racing, I always made a habit of (a) identifying them by large, white writing painted on the panel itself, such as WATER, OIL.P. and OIL.T., etc., and (b) painting a red line on the glass of the dial in the position approximately corresponding to the normal position of the finger of the instrument. In this way, a mere glance is sufficient to make sure, even at night, that everything is normal.

With this arrangement, it is no longer necessary to have the instruments brightly illuminated: they cause less distraction and a better vision of the road is obtained. The all-vital rev-counter is always large enough and sufficiently well provided with red marks not to cause difficulty. Incidentally, when a speedometer is also fitted in addition to the rev-counter, it is a good precaution to mark on its glass the speeds corresponding to the highest permissible engine revolutions in the various gears. This may be useful in case of a rev-counter failure—a not infrequent occurrence.

In my experience, perfect visibility is vitally important wherever fractions of a second are to be saved. In my book, *Starting Grid to Chequered Flag*, I have explained how, driving a D-type Jaguar in a practice session at Silverstone, changing the slightly scratched goggles I had been wearing for a pair of perfect ones, immediately had the effect of cutting down my lap times by 2 to 3 seconds.

If the least possible time is to be lost during the night hours of a race, or on difficult night sections of a rally, the car must have very powerful lighting equipment. For racing, a pair of powerful long-range headlights should be supplemented by two wide-beam fog lights which are not of much use in fog, at racing speeds, but are a great help in illuminating the sides of the road, to enable the driver to place his car correctly on bends. For racing, those auxiliary lights are perhaps even more important than the headlights themselves, as, on a circuit, the driver always knows exactly what lies ahead. If necessary, he can place his car for the next corner before he can actually see it, and he knows his cut-off points which he must, of course, choose so that they are easily recognisable at night. If he does not like the idea of driving at 180 m.p.h. without being able to see the corner at braking distance, then he had better not go to Le Mans, as no headlights available will enable him to do that.

When coming up behind another car, the lights should be dipped, and an anti-glare, two-position driving mirror is most desirable. The dip switch should be very easy to reach and to operate, and it is a good scheme to have it combined with a device enabling the driver to flash the headlights to warn slower cars before they are overtaken. This device should, of course, also be operative during the daylight hours, even with all the lights switched off.

Four powerful front lights, plus all the auxiliaries, will usually use more wattage than the car's dynamo can produce, so if they are used for several hours without interruption, they may run the battery down. An even more serious danger is that the overstressed dynamo should fail. Therefore, the auxiliary lights are better switched off whenever they are not necessary; on a very winding circuit this is hardly possible, but at Le Mans and at Rheims for instance, where they are really useful on only about one-third of the entire circuit, it is a wise precaution to switch them off on the long straights or near-straights, where they do not provide any aid to driving.

The driver who comes into the pits should also remember to switch all lights off, and not to switch them on again before he has restarted the engine, the simultaneous use of four lights and the starter being very hard on the battery.

In their spirit all these recommendations obviously apply to rallying, where the lighting equipment of a car is even more important than for racing. In rallies, the driver usually does not know the road intimately, so that it is essential for him to be able to recognise its shape as early as possible, and well within braking distance, even from quite high speed. That is why, in addition to the head and fog lights, a large powerful long-range spotlamp is a very useful aid to driving on the faster stretches. But again, all the lights should never be switched on simultaneously—nor is there any necessity for doing so, the spotlight being out of place where the fog lights are a help to driving and vice versa.

CHAPTER XI

BECOMING A RACING DRIVER

A RACING career can be started in many different ways and the stories of the rise to fame of the foremost racing drivers would no doubt make interesting and varied reading. Very few of them appeared right out of the blue; for the majority the road leading to the cockpit of a first-class racing car was a long and strenuous one. Lack of money is a major obstacle because a car must be bought somehow, and for many beginners, the main problem is how to make the best of what little money is available. If money is lacking, only extreme determination will lead to the cockpit of a racing car, by which time more than half the battle is won, as that sort of determination also wins races, provided it is intelligently applied. Above all, the technique of race driving, and the car itself, should both be thoroughly understood, in order to extract the utmost from the car and oneself without taking unnecessary risks.

Successful participation in rallies may also eventually lead to circuit racing, but even more time must be devoted to rallying than to racing if success is to be achieved, so that after everything is taken into account, it is quite an expensive way of getting into the game. Moreover, once one has become known as a rally driver, it is very difficult to switch over to proper racing and become accepted as a racing man rather than a rally driver.

In a country like England, where racing at all levels is widespread, hill climbing and club racing seem to be the least expensive ways of getting some racing experience and of finding out if one's ability justifies pressing on with the ambition of becoming a proper racing driver. A car suitable for hill climbing or club racing on a modest scale can be bought comparatively cheaply—secondhand if finance makes it imperative—and the time spent in putting it into proper racing fettle will never be wasted.

Here I would like to venture the opinion that hill climbs,

especially over the short courses used in England, do not provide a very useful sort of practice if one wants to become a proper road racing driver. A few practice runs and one or two timed climbs add up to only a very small mileage, and in racing only mileage produces champions. Hill climbs, however, are won or lost by a few hundredths of a second and are so short that the smallest fraction of time lost anywhere on the course, can never be made up again. Thus the merit of this sort of competition, is to make the driver realise how important it is to place his car with absolute precision, as the slightest error is immediately and irretrievably penalised.

The best way of improving one's ability is to race as much as possible. For a beginner, long races are better than short ones, experience being gained on every lap. Other drivers of known ability should be watched carefully and most of them will only be too pleased to give you advice if you ask them. But do not enter for races in which you or your car would almost surely be hopelessly outclassed. This is asking for trouble and you would only make a nuisance of yourself. Even Formula Junior racing has now become too professional an affair for a beginner to enter, unless he has gained previous experience in other forms of competition or in a racing drivers' school. After all tests have been passed successfully, the better-known racing drivers' schools will agree to enter the best drivers of the course on its own cars in some of the smaller Formula Junior events.

Money spent on a race-driving course or school is never wasted. The least expensive of these organisations are those in which the pupil drives his own car, which should be a reasonably fast vehicle if the course is to be really worth while. These courses usually last for two or three days, which is not long enough for big improvements in one's ability to handle a car to be expected, but during this time much food for thought is given to the participants which they will assimilate over a longer period, when their driving will become progressively better.

Nothing is taught in a race-driving course that a keen and intelligent follower of motor racing could not find out for himself, but such courses can certainly save a lot of time by passing on to a beginner in a few days, what would have taken him much longer to learn from his own experience and observation.

In proper racing schools, the participants usually drive the school's own cars, which makes the course more expensive, but they have the obvious advantage of giving the driver first-hand experience of a real racing car, the handling of which differs more from that of a normal road vehicle—even from a sports car—than is generally realised.

It is therefore not surprising that Gran Turismo racing does not usually produce first-class drivers of small single-seater racing cars. The change from a (usually) closed, comparatively heavy car to a small, open, and very light one calls for a considerable change of style; judgement is notably influenced by the noise that reaches the driver of an open car and by the wind that hits him while, instead of driving the single-seater with his arms, as he did the Gran Turismo, he will have to drive it with his fingertips—both physically and mentally.

That the only really efficient way of learning how to handle a car under racing conditions is actually to race it is obvious, because nowhere other than on a track can the car be driven at its limit and along a line that will enable it to take full advantage of the available width of road. It is surprising how much the judgement of even the most gifted driver with no racing experience, and the accuracy with which he handles his car, will improve with racing practice. On the other hand, I do not agree with those who say that driving on ordinary roads is no help in keeping a driver in racing fettle. True, those highly professional drivers who spend three or four days of nearly every week in the cockpit of a racing car, either racing, practising for races or testing the cars, will benefit much more from some rest while they are away from the tracks than from covering huge mileages on the roads. But I believe that, for a man who races less frequently, to use a fast car on long journeys over fast main roads, especially on the Continent, keeps him in the habit of travelling at high velocities and helps him to maintain his judgement of braking distances and high cornering speeds.

Fast driving on main roads must never be confused with dangerous driving, however, and though they usually average quite phenomenal speeds from point to point, most racing drivers worthy of the name are very safe on the road, where they can call upon a judgement trained at much higher speeds and under more exacting conditions than those prevailing on ordinary roads. Their quest for speed, and their need to express their ability to its utmost, are satisfied by their racing activities, under fully controlled conditions and with a minimum of incidental risks. They can see no reason for taking chances—at crossroads, at blind corners, or in overtaking. After all, if you can hold your own among the pick of the world's racing drivers on the track, there is very little point in trying to match your skill against that of any unknown driver of a family saloon, or even sports car, that you may meet on the road.

Given but moderate ability, they can always leave you behind by taking the sort of chances that must sooner or later end in disaster.

CHAPTER XII

DO'S AND DON'T'S

Do's

START racing at the lowest possible level so that you can assess your own ability compared with other people's and waste the minimum amount of money if there is little hope of getting anywhere.

IF YOU don't prepare your car yourself, spend as much time as you can with the mechanics who prepare it for you, so as to get as much knowledge as possible of its anatomy. Every car has its weak points, and it is best to know what they are so that you may drive accordingly. It may also help you diagnose any possible abnormality in the car's noise or behaviour during the race, and thus to decide whether to stop or to press on.

KEEP AN eye on what other people do before the race and an ear open for what they say, particularly if they are more experienced than you are, and look for interesting details of their cars. They may give you useful hints.

IF YOU are your own manager, write down full details of the practice and race conditions: the lap times, fuel consumption, the state of tune of the car, the gear ratios, the tyre pressures, the kind of fuel and oil used, the oil pressure and temperature, the water temperature during the practice runs and the race, and so on and so forth. These notes may be very useful at a later date, especially if you return to the same circuit with the same car or one which is basically similar.

BEFORE YOU start practising and before the start of the race, make quite sure that someone present in the pits knows your blood group and rhesus.

WEAR LIGHT, narrow shoes. They will help you to operate the pedals with precision.

WHEN YOU set off for the race course, for practice or the race itself, always be prepared for any sort of weather. A thunderstorm comes on quickly, and you will be very unhappy if you don't have waterproofs and a visor handy.

IF YOU have to make a Le Mans start, it is worth practising how to get into the car and get it on its way as quickly as possible. It is essential to find out how much the throttle must be opened for a really quick start of the engine, once it has been previously warmed up. Some quite short races are started the 'Le Mans way' these days, and getting off the mark first or tenth may make quite a considerable difference to the results.

MAKE SURE that the driving position is exactly as you want it; especially if the race is a long one, nothing must be neglected to make yourself really comfortable.

BE SURE to memorise where the ignition switch is, and which way it must be turned to stop the engine should the throttle fail to shut.

MAKE QUITE sure that you can easily identify the instruments and that you know what they should read. If necessary, mark the zone in which the fingers should stand with paint on the dash, so that you can see at first glance if all is well, without having to peer at small figures. This would distract your attention from the road and inevitably ask for trouble or slow you down.

IF IT rains or is likely to rain, wear leather-backed gloves with which your goggles or visor can be easily wiped or, better still sew a small leather on the back of one of the gloves for this purpose.

IF YOU realise that the engine cannot be started in time for the start of the race, raise your arm up, so that the officials, and above all your fellow-drivers, can see that your car will not move and can take action to avoid ramming it.

IF THE starting area is not level, put a small stone or a small piece of wood under a wheel to prevent the car from rolling.

IT IS very easy to over-rev in the first few hundred yards after the start, when you have to watch the other cars running in close attendance rather than the rev-counter and can hardly recognise the sound of your engine from theirs. Take great care that you don't—it may cost you a valve . . . and the race.

DURING THE race, try to drive a little faster than is enjoyable: you cannot go really fast without frightening yourself occasionally.

PAY VERY careful attention to any oil that may have been left on the track by other cars.

IF IT starts to rain, slow down sufficiently not to take any risk, then increase speed progressively as you become familiar with the new state of the track.

WATCH YOUR rear-view mirrors as often as possible and occasionally have a quick glance behind at a hairpin, so as to judge the distance of your followers more accurately.

BE QUITE sure you know the meaning of the various flags, and watch for them during the race.

BE QUITE sure you know the regulations, especially those peculiar to the particular event. It is very important to know the exact starting procedure and the number of people who may work on the car during a pit stop.

GO EARLY to bed the night before the race, and if you feel nervous, don't hesitate to take a sedative in order to get a good night's sleep.

MAKE AN early start to the race. Traffic conditions are likely to be difficult, and having to worry about getting to the start in time will strain your nerves even more than they are before a race anyway.

MAKE SURE you have all the necessary passes to get to the paddock. The arguments that will otherwise ensue will not improve the state of your nerves either.

IF YOU don't know the circuit, try to arrive in time to drive several times round it with a private car before the first practice session starts. This will enable you to take better advantage of the time provided for official practising and you will be less of a nuisance to others who already know their way around. Don't forget to look for possible escape roads during the reconnaissance.

ALWAYS WEAR close-fitting overalls, otherwise the wind will blow them up like balloons and you will feel uncomfortable and look untidy.

USE ONLY two-piece overalls which are much easier to get rid of in case of fire. If possible, have them fire-proofed in a special solution.

FROM THE length of the race and the average speed reached by the fastest cars during practice, calculate the approximate duration of the race. A glance at your watch will then give you a fairly accurate indication of how far the race has progressed. If you are not up amongst the fastest group of competitors, it may also be well worth while calculating how long it will before the leaders are about to lap you, so that you can pay particular attention to keeping out of their way as they close up on you. It's a good way of getting popular with the top men.

Don't's

DON'T DRINK any alcohol with, or after the meal preceding practice or the race, and avoid excessive consumption of alcoholic drinks during the practice and race period.

DON'T EAT more than a light meal before the race.

DON'T FORGET to carry your competitors' licence with you.

DON'T FORGET to take at least one pair of spare goggles and a visor with you, and to leave them with a reliable person in the pits. If any rain is to be expected, don't forget to treat your goggles and visor with an anti-mist compound. Soap is as good as any of them.

DON'T FORGET to inform your team manager or a reliable person in the pit of your blood group and rhesus: this precaution may save your life in case of an accident.

DON'T OMIT to read the race regulations and make sure you know any rule peculiar to the race concerned.

DON'T WAIT until the last moment to wheel, or drive, your car to its proper starting position.

132

DON'T OMIT to keep an accurate check on fuel consumption and tyre wear during practice.

DON'T WAIT until the last moment to start the engine.

DON'T WAIT for too long on the starting line with the clutch depressed.

DON'T FORGET properly to adjust your driving mirrors before the start.

DON'T PULL your goggles down too early: they may mist up.

DON'T WEAR over-warm clothing. Once in the race, you will always get warmer than you had thought. Don't wear waterproofs unless it is raining or likely to rain very hard: otherwise they will be unbearably hot.

DON'T FORGET to tell the people responsible for your signalling what sort of information you will be particularly interested in receiving.

DON'T GET in the way of faster competitors, but when they have overtaken you, try to keep up with them as long as you can and watch their methods closely: you can learn a lot this way.

DON'T TAKE anything a racing driver says for granted. Even the most reliable ones can only say what they *think* they do. If one tells you he takes a bend flat-out with a car similar to yours, and you do not, never try to do what he says without building up progressively to it. If he tells you he brakes at the 200 yards sign for a corner, try first at 300, then 250 and then reduce your distance progressively if you see it really can be done. Drivers usually consider they have reached a landmark when they see it at about 45 degrees to the car's centreline, not when they get level with it, which makes quite a difference. In addition, their instinct of preservation makes them apply the brakes a fraction of a second earlier than they actually think they do.

To do what a racing driver says he does without building up to it progressively, is the quickest way of getting killed.

IF YOU decide to change your line through a fast bend, never do so without first trying the new line at a slightly reduced speed, to see if it is really better. It may be worse, in which case, you will be glad you reduced your speed. Only by sheer luck did I avoid a very nasty crash, at about 100 m.p.h., by not observing this rule in one of my first big races.

DON'T CHANGE gear unnecessarily. Every gear change costs nearly a car's length, so it may be better to stay in a higher gear than to change down to get momentarily better acceleration, and then change up again. In case of doubt, always stay in the higher gear, you will be faster and strain the car less.

DON'T DRIVE any faster than is necessary to achieve the best possible result you can hope for, while keeping a reasonable safety margin over the closest competitor. Of course, this can mean driving as fast as you possibly can all the way!

IN A long-distance race, never eat anything heavy while waiting for your turn at the wheel, and get as much rest as possible. Before you resume driving, make quite sure of your car's position in the race, and how far in front or behind your most dangerous opponents are.

WHEN HANDING over to your co-driver, don't forget to inform him of any abnormality in the car that has come to your notice, especially where the brakes are concerned, and also report them to the team or pit manager.

NEVER WEAR any item of nylon clothing or clothing of similar material that will melt in the case of a fire.

BANKING ANGLE AND TYRE LOAD

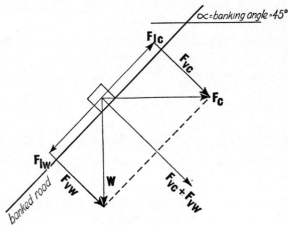

Figure 59

LET us assume that, for a given radius of the curve, the centrifugal force F_c is equal to the weight W of the vehicle. In this case, if the lateral components created by these two forces are to cancel each other out, as happens if the car is driven along the correct line around the banked curve, the banking angle must be 45 degrees (see fig. 59).

We have

$$F_c = \frac{mv^2}{r},$$

v being the speed of the car in ft./sec,
r being the radius of the curve.

But we have assumed that $F_c = W$, and $W = mg$,
m being the mass of the vehicle, and
g being the acceleration of gravity.

For F_c to be equal to W, we must have

$$\frac{mv^2}{r} = mg, \text{ and } \frac{v^2}{r} = g.$$

Thus

$$v^2 = rg.$$

Under these circumstances, the force with which the car bears upon the road surface is

$$F_{vc} + F_{vw} = F_c \sin \alpha + W \sin \alpha = \sin \alpha \ (F_c + W).$$

As in our case, $\alpha = 45°$ and $F_c = W$, we have

$$F_{vc} + F_{vw} = 0 \cdot 71 \times 2W = 1 \cdot 42 W.$$

The total force with which the car bears upon the track is thus $1 \cdot 42$ times its own weight.

* * *

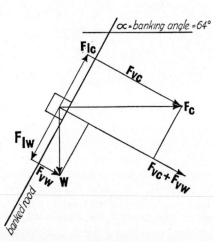

Figure 60

Let us now assume that the car's speed is increased to the extent that the centrifugal force F_c becomes twice the car's weight: $F_c = 2W$, and let us calculate what the banking angle will have to be for F_{lw} and F_{lc} to be equal (see fig. 60).

We have

$$\cos \alpha = \frac{F_{lc}}{F_c},$$

$$\sin \alpha = \frac{F_{lw}}{W}.$$

As $F_c = 2W$ and $F_{lw} = F_{lc}$, we have

$$\cos \alpha = \frac{F_{lw}}{2W}, \text{ and sine } \alpha = 2 \cos \alpha.$$

It follows that

$$\sin^2 \alpha = 4 \cos^2 \alpha. \tag{1}$$

By definition,

$$\sin^2 \alpha = 1 - \cos^2 \alpha. \tag{2}$$

Subtracting (2) from (1), we have

$$4 \cos^2 \alpha - 1 + \cos^2 \alpha = 0, \text{ or } 5 \cos^2 \alpha = 1.$$

Thus

$$\cos^2 \alpha = \tfrac{1}{5} = 0 \cdot 20,$$

$$\cos \alpha = \sqrt{0 \cdot 2} \simeq 0 \cdot 45$$

and $\alpha = 64$ degrees.

Thus, for the sideway forces acting upon the vehicle to cancel each other out, when the centrifugal force F_c is twice the car's weight, the banking must be inclined at 64 degrees to the horizontal.

As $F_c = 2W = 2mg$,

$$\frac{v^2}{2r} = g \text{ and } v^2 = 2rg.$$

$$v^2 = 19 \cdot 6r, \text{ and } v = \sqrt{19 \cdot 6r}.$$

At this speed, and at the correct banking angle of $\alpha = 64$ degrees, the component of the centrifugal force acting perpendicularly to the road surface is

$$F_{vc} = F_c \sin \alpha = 2W \sin \alpha \simeq 1 \cdot 8W;$$

and the component of the weight acting perpendicularly to the road surface is

$$F_{vw} = W \cos \alpha \simeq 0 \cdot 45W.$$

137

The total force with which the car bears upon the road is thus

$$F_{vc} + F_{vw} = W\ (2\ \sin\ \alpha + \cos\ \alpha) = 2\cdot 25\,W$$

or $2\cdot 25$ times its own weight, in the circumstances described.
This condition is reached at a speed of approximately 157 m.p.h.

INDEX

INDEX

The numerals in heavy type refer to the *figure numbers* of illustrations

141